Navigating Initial Teach Training

Are you considering or already training to become a teacher?

Do you want to know more about the variety of types of training on offer?

Do you need reassurance that you are on the right path?

Or would you just like to see how others cope with their teacher training?

If so, this lively book, built on the experience of thousands of people just like you, is exactly what you need. Written by experts with backgrounds in teaching, supporting teacher learning and researching teacher training, and based on a major study of nearly 5,000 beginner teachers, it provides an authentic insight into what lies ahead when becoming a teacher.

The book, which incorporates extensive conversations with large numbers of student and newly qualified teachers, will also serve as the ideal course companion when undertaking your initial teacher training programme. It includes practical ideas and strategies for coping with various aspects of life as a student teacher, such as dealing with pupil behaviour, building and managing relationships with mentors and other teachers in schools, and finding and obtaining a first teaching post.

Andrew J. Hobson is Associate Professor in the Teacher and Leadership Research Centre (TLRC) in the School of Education at the University of Nottingham. He has previously worked as a teacher and as a Senior Research Officer at the National Foundation for Educational Research (NFER).

Angi Malderez is an Education Consultant, prior to which she was Senior Lecturer in the School of Education at the University of Leeds. She has worked as a teacher, a teacher of teachers (ToT) and a teacher of ToTs in the UK, Asia, South America, Africa and Europe.

Louise Tracey is a Research Fellow at the Institute for Effective Education at the University of York. Prior to this she worked as a researcher at the University of Nottingham and the University of Liverpool.

Navigating Initial Teacher Training

Becoming a teacher

Andrew J. Hobson,
Angi Malderez and
Louise Tracey

Routledge
Taylor & Francis Group

LONDON AND NEW YORK

First published 2009
by Routledge
2 Park Square, Milton Park, Abingdon, Oxon, OX14 4RN

Simultaneously published in the USA and Canada
by Routledge
270 Madison Avenue, New York, NY 10016

Routledge is an imprint of the Taylor & Francis Group, an informa business

Typeset in Garamond by Prepress Projects Ltd, Perth, UK
Printed and bound in Great Britain by TJ International Ltd, Padstow, Cornwall

British Library Cataloguing in Publication Data
A catalogue record for this book is available from the British Library

Library of Congress Cataloging in Publication Data
Hobson, Andy, 1965–
Navigating initial teacher training / Andrew J. Hobson, Angi Malderez & Louise Tracey.
p. cm.
Includes bibliographical references and index.
1. Teachers–Training of. I. Malderez, Angi, 1950– II. Tracey, Louise. III. Title.
LB1707.H63 2009
370.71–dc22
2008044009

ISBN10: 0-415-43333-9 (hbk)
ISBN10: 0-415-43334-7 (pbk)

ISBN13: 978-0-415-43333-4 (hbk)
ISBN13: 978-0-415-43334-1 (pbk)

Contents

Acknowledgements

The research ('Becoming a Teacher') upon which this book is based was carried out on behalf of, and funded by, the Department for Children, Schools and Families (DCSF), the General Teaching Council for England (GTCE) and the Training and Development Agency for Schools (TDA). We would like to thank all members of the 'Becoming a Teacher' research team (at the Universities of Nottingham and Leeds, and Ipsos MORI Social Research Institute) and all members of the project Steering Group for their valuable contributions to the research. Last but certainly not least, we are particularly indebted to the (then) student and newly qualified teachers who gave up valuable time to participate in the research.

Introduction

This book is about making the decision to undertake a programme of initial teacher training (ITT) and then what it feels like to do so. It is informed by a large-scale research study of the experiences of people who have trained to become teachers on different kinds of ITT programmes.

We, the authors, imagine writers (in this case, *us*) and their readers (*you*) as engaged in a kind of 'dialogue at a distance'. For any dialogue to go well and participants to get a sense of satisfaction and achievement, certain conditions need to be met. These include the need for all participants to have a sense of why they are 'talking' and what they hope to achieve, and for everyone to know something about each other and be 'talking the same language'. We therefore aim in this first chapter to contribute to creating a context for successful dialogue. We begin by describing who we imagine you the readers will be, and why we think you might want to read on, as well as introducing ourselves and our reasons for writing this book. We then discuss what is (and is not) discussed in the book, and provide an outline of the content of each of the chapters. Next, we include a note about some of the language we use (where we think there could be different ways of understanding what we write that might cause breakdowns in the dialogue). Finally, we suggest some ways you might like to use this book.

Who the book is for

We have written this book primarily for two groups of people. The first group is people who are *considering* undertaking an initial teacher training (ITT) programme. If you belong to this group you may have many questions on your mind as you consider your options. For example, you may be asking yourself:

- What is it like to experience an ITT programme?
- How do I decide if undertaking an ITT programme is a good idea for me?
- Would I fit in with my fellow trainees?[1]
- How have others made their decisions to start a programme?
- Am I suited to do this course?

Or it may be that you have decided that you do want to train to be a teacher but can't decide which of a range of different types of programmes that lead to qualified teacher status (QTS) would be the best for you. If you are asking yourself these kinds of questions, then this book will help you think them through as you make these important decisions.

The second group of people we are writing for includes those of you who have already made these decisions and are about to start, or have already started, an ITT programme. If you belong to this group, this book may be seen and used as a 'course companion', which will provide you with reassurance as well as practical ideas and strategies for coping with various aspects of life as a trainee teacher. The kinds of questions and thoughts such readers might bring to the dialogue include:

- How will certain aspects of my programme help me become a (good) teacher?
- How can I get on better with my mentor?
- How can I get pupils to behave more appropriately?
- Is teaching really for me?
- Will I ever feel like a proper teacher?
- What can I do to help myself secure a teaching post?

To summarise, we are primarily writing for and to student teachers (including people thinking about becoming a student teacher), and when we write 'you' in this text we are thinking of these two main groups of readers.

Three further groups of readers might also find this book useful and of interest. The first includes those who support the learning of people becoming teachers. Teachers of teachers (ToTs) might find the research-based student teacher perspective on the lived experience of undertaking ITT, which we present, both informative and useful for their own practice, and supportive for the student teachers they work with. The second further group of potential readers are postgraduate (e.g. MA/PhD) students who are studying or researching 'teacher education', and the third group comprises policy-makers whose remit includes responsibility for the initial training of beginning teachers. Again, these last two groups may be interested to read about the lived and felt experiences of those who have been through the ITT process, and may be interested to read about some of the strategies that we (the authors) propose to help student teachers to navigate different aspects of their ITT journey.

Finally, although the research study on which this book is based was conducted in England in the first decade of the twenty-first century (see the Appendix for details of our 'Becoming a Teacher' research), we know from other studies internationally that the majority of the themes and issues discussed in the following chapters are common to the experiences of student teachers elsewhere in the world.[2] We believe therefore that this book should interest and be useful to people involved with initial teacher training programmes in different parts of the world, whether they (you) are student teachers (or potential student teachers), ITT tutors or mentors, or policy-makers.

Who the authors are and why we wrote this book

The first two authors of this book have undergone the experience you are contemplating or undergoing yourselves – that is, we have undertaken ITT courses and subsequently gone on to work as qualified teachers in schools and colleges. After a time teaching, we have both also worked as teachers of both beginner and more experienced teachers. All three authors have had the more recent experience of talking to a large number of student teachers (in England) about their experiences of ITT, and analysing the responses to a range of questions from an even larger group of student teachers who took part in a survey about ITT. This was in the context of a research study (the 'Becoming a Teacher' project) that sought to understand the experiences of student teachers who were following a range of different kinds of ITT programmes with the aim of becoming either primary school or secondary school teachers.[3] We are using what these student teachers told us, and our understanding of it, as the starting points for the different chapters and discussions in the book. In fact, the title of each of the following chapters begins with a quotation from one of the student teachers we spoke to (though the quotations are not necessarily representative of the views of all trainees!).

We have learnt a lot from the student teachers who gave up their time to talk to us and respond to the surveys about what it is like to become and be a student teacher, and we believe that others will also benefit from what the student teachers in our study had to say. One reason for writing the book, therefore, is to provide those who might be most interested – the next generations of student teachers – with easy access to the experiences and views of the trainees (or ex-trainees) in our study. In doing this, we create another dialogue – between you and the student teachers whose views and words we report.

What the book is and is not

We intend this book to be a source of information and support as you (prospective and actual student teachers) make your initial decisions to undertake ITT and/or as you navigate your experience of ITT. Our research study has allowed us to understand something of the various complex motivations of our research participants, all of whom had made the decision to become a student teacher and were enrolled on various types of ITT programme. We describe these in Section 1 of the book. Becoming aware of the kinds of reasoning many other student teachers have used to arrive at their decisions will help those contemplating embarking on an ITT programme not only in deciding whether or not to train as a teacher, but also in deciding which type of ITT programme might suit them best.

Becoming a teacher is not just about the development of subject knowledge, about developing strategies for classroom and behaviour management, and about meeting the occupational Standards or 'competencies', as some may perhaps think. Our research, based on extensive conversations with a large number of student and beginning teachers, together with our own experience of becoming teachers and training teachers, shows that becoming a teacher and successfully navigating a programme of ITT:

- is fundamentally about developing a teacher identity – of coming to think of yourself *as* a teacher; and in part because of this
- is inevitably an emotionally charged journey littered with both 'highs' and 'lows'; and
- is dependent perhaps more than any other single factor on the development of effective, meaningful and productive relationships with your mentors, with other teachers in your placement schools and (last but certainly not least) with the pupils in the classes you are charged to teach (to help learn).

What this book does *not* do is deal directly with specific aspects of student teacher learning such as subject knowledge development, or the development of knowledge and skills to implement appropriate teaching methods (or methods of facilitating learning). Rather, by giving more attention to the equally important personal aspects of being a student teacher, we aim to complement ITT programmes (and other books on the subject) that do address such issues.

A main aim of the book is to provide those contemplating enrolling on an ITT programme with a picture of what the experience is likely to feel like, and, for those who are already student teachers, to suggest a range of strategies for managing different aspects of their experience and to provide answers to some of the questions they are likely to ask.

How the book is organised

Although in some respects now may not be the time to say this (you may not want to hear it!), there is a sense in which you are starting (or contemplating starting) a learning journey that will not end with the end of your ITT programme. It may be comforting to know, however, that in many ways the journey also started long before this point in time or before you contemplated your decision about whether or not to undertake an ITT programme. So, although this book deals mainly with that part of the journey you may or will make as student teachers, the focus of Section 1 is on what you bring to your ITT programme. The subsequent sections of the book focus on different aspects and key stages of the journey undertaken by student teachers, a journey that can be enlightening, rewarding and fun on the one hand, yet tempestuous, frustrating and very hard work on the other! If you choose or have already chosen to undertake the ITT voyage, this book will help you to navigate the enticing yet potentially stormy waters you will encounter. Below we briefly outline the main issues discussed in each of the following chapters.

Section 1: Thinking about training to be a teacher

Chapter 1 'I just fancied the challenge': is teaching for you?

In this chapter we encourage you to consider what might attract you to teaching, what might deter you from becoming a teacher, and whether you possess (or can develop) the qualities and skills necessary for becoming an effective teacher. We also prompt you to consider whether you might be better suited to teaching in primary schools (teaching children between the ages of 4/5 and 11) or secondary schools (11–16/18).

Chapter 2 'It was the easiest and the quickest!': choosing an ITT route and provider

In this chapter we raise a number of considerations that you might usefully think about before you come to a decision about which ITT route you would prefer to follow and which institution or providers (if you have a choice) you would prefer to be trained by (assuming that you first choose to undertake an ITT programme). To help you think this through, we describe those issues that have actually impacted upon student teachers' choices of ITT route and provider.

Chapter 3 'You build teachers up into these god-like people who are fantastic and amazing and how will you ever be that perfect?': preparing to make the most of your ITT

In this chapter we seek to encourage those of you who are going to train to become a teacher to uncover and develop your existing ideas about teaching and teacher training, with a view to helping you to make the most of (or get the most out of) your ITT. We do this by encouraging you to think about what you are looking forward to about ITT, what you might be concerned about, and what you need to learn and how you think you might best learn it. We end the chapter by passing on the advice given by the student teachers in our research to anyone considering undertaking an ITT course.

Section 2: Being a student teacher

Chapter 4 'It's all a bit overwhelming at first!': dealing with the emotional roller-coaster of beginning a teacher training course

The early stages of a teacher training course, especially being in schools and having contact with pupils for the first time, can be a difficult, highly emotional and stressful period for many student teachers, for whom it is often predominantly a case of 'survival'. In this chapter we discuss some of the common sources of worry, frustration and unhappiness that those beginning an ITT course might encounter, and some of the strategies that have been and might be employed for dealing with 'lows' in general and with specific lows in particular. If at this stage of your ITT you feel that you are on an emotional roller-coaster, you will be reassured that you are not alone, and encouraged to recognise some of the positives that you might take from your experiences.

Chapter 5 'It wears you down emotionally': dealing with issues of pupil behaviour

This chapter addresses one of the major sources of anxiety and emotional 'lows' encountered by student teachers, that relating to pupil behaviour. We emphasise that not *all* pupils behave inappropriately, that part of the job of your ITT tutors and mentors is to help you develop appropriate skills of behaviour management, and that many student teachers complete their ITT programmes feeling that their ability to manage pupil behaviour is a strength. We also recognise, however, that some pupils do behave inappropriately some of the time, and we offer both a number of ways of thinking about pupil behaviour and a number of practical strategies that we hope those of you who encounter inappropriate behaviour in your classrooms will find helpful.

Chapter 6 'All the theory goes out of the window'?: the relevance and value of theory in ITT

Many student teachers fail to understand the relevance of some aspects of their ITT, notably those elements referred to as 'theory'. This chapter discusses student teachers' perceptions of the relevance and value of 'theory' in ITT, and makes suggestions for how you can manage your learning in ways which may help you to recognise the relevance, value and practical utility of theory, and to create coherence in your learning experiences.

Chapter 7 'I'm glad I've built up such good relationships': building and maintaining productive relationships in ITT

Student teachers' accounts of both positive and negative experiences during teacher training are replete with references to their relationships with a range of significant others, including their school-based mentors, other teachers in schools and pupils in their teaching groups. As well as highlighting the important role of relationships within the student teacher learning process, and showing that trainees who may be encountering relationship issues are not alone, this chapter (building on suggestions for forming productive relationships given in Chapter 3) suggests a number of strategies for building and maintaining good relationships, and for resolving interpersonal conflicts.

Chapter 8 'I can't be doing with it': are you thinking of quitting ITT?

Every year, many student teachers make the decision to withdraw from their initial teacher training programmes. This chapter discusses the reasons for these decisions and what those student teachers who withdrew from their programmes felt might have helped them to complete their ITT. These ideas form the basis of a number of suggested strategies for dealing both with difficulties experienced and the difficult decision about whether or not to withdraw. The chapter also suggests that student teachers experiencing difficulties in their training and/or their personal circumstances might rethink whether their situations are as problematic as they first thought, or might consider the option of deferring completion of their ITT rather than withdrawing completely.

Section 3: Moving beyond initial teacher training and looking ahead

Chapter 9 'I just got this feeling when I walked in, I felt that I would fit there': finding and securing your first teaching post

In this chapter we discuss a range of issues associated with applying for teaching posts. Drawing on our research findings and our own experience both of gaining and of appointing people to teaching posts, we offer a number of suggestions to help you decide what type of post you are looking for and to help you secure your first post as a newly qualified teacher.

Conclusion: 'Ditching the student teacher tag'

In our short, concluding chapter, we restate some of the key points we have made in the book and briefly discuss some of the things that those who are about to embark on their first year as qualified teachers have to look forward to.

A note about language and terminology

Although we seek to explain the terms that we use in this book as we go along, we have also included a Glossary, which can be found towards the back of the book, to help explain the meaning of some of the technical or specialist terms that you will come across in the book and are associated with ITT courses. We want to mention here, however, that some of the terms referred to in the book and in ITT are *contested*. Because of this, you will find that different writers or teacher educators will: (1) use different terms for essentially the same idea, or to refer to the same thing; and (2) use the same term to mean something different! So, if you find yourself reading about something here that you would use a different word to describe, or you have heard (or read) someone else using a different word to describe, you might like to ask yourself why. One possible answer might be that we are using a more technical or 'professional' language; part of your learning on your ITT programmes will be to learn both the language of teachers and, to the extent that it is different, the academic language of education. Another part of your learning will be to understand the professional meanings behind 'ordinary' language, such as, for example, 'learning' or 'teaching'. Having said all that, we are conscious that you are starting this learning and we have tried not to use too much technical language or to use ordinary language in technical ways without explaining that we are doing so and what we mean.

Ways of using the book

We see three main reasons you (potential or actual student teachers) might want to use this book, or chapters in it:

- to make initial decisions, for example about which ITT route to choose;
- to prepare yourself, emotionally and practically, for example for being a student teacher or for finding a first job;
- to trouble-shoot and find ideas for strategies to help you deal with specific situations that student teachers experience, for example problematic relationships with mentors or others.

If you are using the book on your own

If you are thinking about becoming a student teacher, you may want to focus mostly on Section 1. However, reading through the other sections would also help you to get a good feel for what you might expect to encounter on an ITT course, which would also be useful in helping you make up your mind.

If you are already a student teacher, we think that this would be a useful book to read all the way through at or near the start of your programme, so that you can make decisions about strategies you might find comfortable to use, and plan for those aspects of your experience in which 'starting right' is important (such as in building your relationships with others). You might also like to keep it handy throughout your programme both as a comforting reminder that you are not alone and as a useful resource for trouble-shooting when/if you encounter difficulties.

If you are using the book in a group

There are many ways this book could be used in informal or formal groups. The suggestions that follow are largely for small informal groups of student teachers. And if you do form such a group you might well be providing an important additional source of support for each other!

Reading group

Such a group might agree to take a particular chapter and read it before meeting and using it as the basis for discussions.

Survey group

You could as a group, and focusing on one chapter at a time, ask each other the questions that frequently appear at the beginning of chapters, and compare and discuss similarities and differences between group members' responses. You could then go on to read the full chapter and compare your own and the group's responses with those given by the student teachers in our research. The next step would be to see and discuss whether, and if so how and why, your responses might differ or your views might have changed.

Trying-out group

You could agree as a group to try out in schools the same suggested practical strategy on a particular issue and report back to each other about what happened. Or you might agree to each try a different suggestion, again reporting back to your group about what happened and discussing the all important 'why?' and 'what now?' questions. (See Chapter 6 for a process you could use to help you learn further from your experience.)

To conclude this introduction, it remains only for us to say that, however you use it and whatever your motives for reading it, we hope you will enjoy the book and find it helpful.

Thinking about training to be a teacher

'I just fancied the challenge'

Is teaching for you?

Introduction

Before deciding whether or not to become a teacher, or indeed before deciding whether or not to follow any particular employment path, it is important that you consider your decision carefully, that you have a good insight into what the job entails, and that you have thought about how well you as an individual might be suited to the job, or to different variations of the job, such as (in the case of teaching) whether to work in a primary or a secondary school. This chapter will help you to decide whether or not teaching might be for you, or, if you have already decided to become a teacher, will allow you to reflect on that decision, by providing insights into the thinking and reasoning of a large number of people who have previously made the decision to undertake a teacher training (ITT) course.

In this chapter we discuss the kinds of questions that it will be helpful for you to think about, and we also describe how the people in our research study reasoned about each question. Before that though, we want to say that the main thing our research revealed was that, for each individual, the reasons behind the decision to train as a teacher were unique personal combinations of factors. So, for example, if you read later in this chapter that the majority of people in our study gave reason X as part of their motivation for training to be teacher, and reason X does not seem to be true for you, this does not necessarily mean that you are not suited to teaching. It will still be helpful to reflect on the reasons given by the people in our study to help you think about yourself and your own decision about whether or not to train to become a teacher. More generally, it will be valuable for you to consider your responses, and the strength of your responses, to each of the following important questions:

- How much do you want or need to change your current situation?
- How attractive is teaching to you and why?
- Do you have reservations about teaching as a career and, if so, how 'big' or important are they to you?
- How confident are you that you will make an effective teacher?

The first two questions that it might be helpful for you to think about are both connected to your motivation for undertaking teacher training. We start with the question relating to how, to what extent and why your current situation is 'pushing' you into making a change, before considering what might be 'pulling' you towards training as a teacher. If you can identify a number of 'pull', or both 'push' and 'pull', reasons for yourself, then you are likely to have the kind of robust motivation that will help you through the demands of your training and beyond. The next question we discuss relates to reservations you may have about teaching. Thinking these through carefully and comparing them with your motivation can be a useful reality check.

Finally, although we would say that teachers are 'made' (given sufficient time, appropriate circumstances and support) rather than 'born', it will be helpful, in making the initial decision about whether or not to train as a teacher, to assess whether you already have some of what it takes to be a teacher. This will require that you think carefully about *yourself* – your personality, your likes and dislikes, and what you have already learnt – and whether this might mean that (with training) you could be an effective teacher. (You might even ask other people who know you what they think about all this.) Thinking about these issues might also be advantageous for other reasons. First, if you conclude that you do already possess some relevant knowledge and/or skills to be a teacher then this can be a confidence-booster, and realistic confidence will be helpful for both your learning and your teaching should you make the decision to undertake an ITT programme. Second, having an understanding of what you bring to your learning teaching journey (and of what you need to learn during that journey) may help you decide what type of training may be most suited to you (see Chapter 2). Third, thinking all of this through is useful preparation for the interview you would probably need to undergo in order to secure a place on an ITT course.

How much do you want or need to change your current situation?

For some readers, perhaps those of you who have just finished or are about to complete your A-levels or an undergraduate degree, this question may not seem so appropriate, as you may have completed one phase of study/ life and may be considering whether you will undertake a further period of study or enter the world of work. Undertaking an ITT course is a method of combining these two considerations, although, as we will see in Chapter 2, some ITT programmes tend to place more emphasis on study whereas others place more emphasis on work (and learning 'on the job').

Some readers will already have entered the world of work but will be considering a change of career. You may be in the position of some of the participants in our research study who, having had various occupations, decided for various reasons that it was time for a change and, partly because of the variety of ways to train as a teacher that now exist (see Chapter 2), were able to take the decision to train as teachers.

So what kinds of reasons might prompt people to want to change from one career to teaching? Some of the reasons given by participants in our study related to dissatisfaction with aspects of their current jobs. These included:

- not enjoying their jobs, or feeling unhappy and/or stressed in their work;
- feeling that their work was not sufficiently rewarding or challenging;
- feeling that they had insufficient job security or promotion prospects;
- not getting on very well with or having much in common with work colleagues;
- feeling that aspects of their current employment they particularly enjoyed would be more prominent in a teaching career.

These various reasons are illustrated in the following quotations from some of the student teachers that we talked to:

> [A]fter all those previous years of getting nowhere, and I was getting really stressed out that I wasn't feeling useful, not having a profession as such, you know . . . not belonging in a way.
>
> (Female, 20–24, primary)[1]

> I came to a point where scientific research is great but you're always working on short-term contracts and there's very little opportunity for career progression so I was looking around for a new career.
>
> (Female, 40–44, secondary)

> I got into manufacturing and stores management . . . I worked on despatch and assembly. The thing that kept me actually interested in the job was that I used to train people on PCs and general things. That was the only thing that kept me there.
>
> (Male, 30–34, primary)

Finally, many trainees indicated in their responses to our survey and in the interviews that they were influenced by a range of practical or pragmatic reasons, including whether or not being a teacher would fit in with their personal circumstances or family lives, to which we return shortly.

> [L]ast year I only had two days' holiday together because if I wasn't there nobody would do my job. And also I'd decided that if I did want

to have a family then being in the car at seven o'clock every day to drive into [City], and law is not a family-friendly business anyway, was not really what I wanted to do.

(Female, 25–29, secondary)

I've got three young children so family and work/life balance was a big issue and really that was more important than money . . . I'd earn a bit less but I'd get a good [work/life] balance on that.

(Male, 30–34, primary)

And I've got children, so every way I looked at it teaching suited me . . . then when you look at the career progression possibilities, the hours that you work, how close to home you can work, the holidays that you get, with having children of my own, great, everything fitted.

(Male, 35–39, primary)

If you have definitely decided that you need to change your current circumstances, and that training as a teacher is one of your options, then you need to consider carefully the second of our two main 'motivation' questions, to which we now turn.

How attractive is teaching to you and why?

If you have this book in your hands and have read this far, something is making you think that teaching might be a good choice of career for you. Before you read on, you might like to make a list of all the things about teaching that makes it attractive to you as a career choice to compare with the responses of the student teachers in our study.

In our survey we asked almost 5,000 student teachers to what extent (if at all) they were attracted to undertaking an ITT programme by a wide range of possible reasons. In Table 1.1 we list the 12 factors which attracted the highest numbers of survey respondents. As you can see, the biggest single response was 'helping young people to learn', which 98 per cent of all respondents said had attracted them to teaching, and over three-quarters (78 per cent) said had 'strongly attracted' them. This, together with some of the other considerations, such as wanting to give something back to the community or wanting to teach pupils better than you had been taught yourself, might be referred to as an *altruistic* motive for becoming a teacher. And in our interviews we did come across many trainees who were attracted to teaching because they wanted to 'make a difference', such as the trainee whom we quote below:

It's nice to be part of people's growing up. I look back at my teachers and I still remember the ones that I loved at primary school. I remember the impact they made on my life . . . I'd like to be able to give that to children, that sort of enjoyment and the amount of pleasure I got out of it . . . I'd love to think that fifteen years down the line somebody would say that about me.

(Female, 30–34, primary)

Some of the considerations which attracted many people to teaching are factors that are *intrinsic* to the occupation, such as 'working with children or young people' (is this for you?), 'the challenging nature of the job' (do you like a challenge?), 'the professional status of teaching' (are you attracted by the idea of having a profession?) and 'collegiality/teamwork aspects of teaching' (do you like working as part of a team?). Other influential factors for many student teachers in our study, and ones that you should also consider, are often referred to as *extrinsic* factors, and these include the 'long holidays' associated with teaching compared with many other jobs, and the 'job security' and 'opportunities for career development' that teaching

Table 1.1 Factors attracting student teachers to ITT

	Strongly attracted (%)	Moderately attracted (%)	Total attracted (%)
Helping young people to learn	78	20	98
Working with children or young people	59	33	92
Being inspired by a good teacher	48	36	84
Giving something back to the community	33	46	79
The challenging nature of the job	29	48	77
Job security	24	45	69
Long holidays	26	42	68
The professional status of teaching	19	44	63
Opportunities for career development	19	44	63
Staying involved with a subject specialism	25	32	57
Wanting to teach pupils better than in own experience	22	35	57
Collegiality/teamwork aspects of teaching	11	46	57

might provide. With regard to 'long holidays', it can be beneficial in various ways if as a parent you are able to share the same vacation period with your children. On the other hand, many teachers will tell you that at least some of your holiday time will inevitably be spent working at home.

Two other extrinsic factors that did not make the 'top twelve' attractions but nevertheless attracted a significant minority of trainees in our survey are 'teacher salary' (which 41 per cent of respondents said attracted them to teaching) and the 'benefits package (e.g. occupational pension)' associated with teaching, which each attracted 29 per cent of respondents. It would be wise to investigate both of these issues, and how each of them compares with other occupations, and with your own expectations, aspirations and needs in terms of your future income. Many of you will have mortgages to pay, many of you will be bringing up or considering bringing up children, and you may be (or may become) the main or sole wage-earner in your family for the foreseeable future.

Further (and up-to-date) information on teachers' pay and benefits in England can be found on the TDA website: www.tda.gov.uk/Recruit/lifeasateacher/payandbenefits/salaryscales.aspx. For more information on teachers' pensions see www.teacherspensions.co.uk. For those planning to teach in other countries, government websites may provide similar information.

Primary or secondary teaching?

Some readers considering a career in teaching may be undecided about whether primary or secondary school teaching would suit them better. Amongst our survey participants, although the ideas of 'working with children or young people' and 'helping young people to learn' were more attractive than any of the other factors listed in the questionnaire to trainees seeking to teach both in primary and secondary schools, there were some subtle differences between the reasons given for undertaking ITT by these two groups. First, a relatively higher proportion of primary trainees (82 per cent) than those seeking to teach in secondary schools (74 per cent) stated that they were strongly attracted by 'helping young people to learn', and 72 per cent of primary phase trainees stated that they were strongly attracted to 'working with children or young people', compared with a relatively low 45 per cent of secondary trainees.

In contrast, a higher proportion (41 per cent) of those who were training to teach in secondary schools (where teachers tend to specialise in the teaching of one or two subjects) were strongly attracted by the idea of 'staying involved with a subject specialism', compared with a relatively low 10 per cent of those training to teach in the primary sector (in which teachers are typically involved with a broader range of subjects).

Those of you who are considering becoming a teacher and wondering whether primary or secondary teaching would suit you better might also reflect on whether you prefer to work with and spend more time with women (who are normally in the majority amongst primary school teachers) and younger children, on the one hand, or both men and women and older pupils/learners (including teenagers!), on the other. Prospective male teachers might also bear in mind that, whereas the majority of primary school teachers are women, a proportionately higher number of men (rightly or wrongly!) progress to be head teachers, some in a relatively short time period. Some of the trainees we spoke to talked about the importance to them of some of these considerations:

> [I preferred] primary [teaching] just because that age I think is critical. If you lose them very young, you never get them back.
>
> (Female, 25–29, primary)

> I didn't want to have to cope with stroppy teenagers . . . that was my main consideration really, I wouldn't have to worry about that. Also I loved the idea of the variety, the different subjects.
>
> (Female, 20–24, primary)

> I loved history so I decided that I'd prefer to actually teach one topic and decided that I lacked the creativity for primary school teaching. I think the constant sugar paper and displays would have worn me down so I decided that probably secondary school was where I wanted to go and teach history.
>
> (Female, 25–29, secondary)

> [I] can see myself developing my career to being a] deputy head, head, head of department, whatever…to get some promotion . . . and there is a bit of me that knows that as a man I have a better chance of that because it is kind of a sexist system and I like that in a way, it gives me a better chance. When I talk to people they say there is a good chance of you being a deputy head in five or six years' time, great, you know, head in ten years' time, great. It is a reasonable possibility.
>
> (Male, 35–39, primary)

Finally, you might bear in mind too that some teacher training qualifications also enable you to gain experience of and 'qualify' you to teach in sixth-form colleges and further education institutions, although there are separate courses for those who prefer to teach in post-compulsory education.[2]

Do you have reservations about teaching as a career and, if so, how 'big' or important are they to you?

In any decision-making it is important to consider the 'cons' as well as the 'pros', so that you make a stronger and more realistic decision. In order to think about what the possible drawbacks to training as a teacher might be, you can draw on your own experience of being in school as a learner, and talk to as many teachers as you can. If you have not already done this, getting into schools and spending some time there – maybe volunteering to help in some way – is advisable because it can help you to identify and help you establish how strongly you feel about various pros and cons. If you are undecided about whether primary or secondary teaching is for you, try to spend some time in both types of school, and ideally more than one of each. Not all schools are the same. You might feel uncomfortable in some schools and this could put you off teaching (or primary or secondary schools), but you might feel 'at home' and 'this is for me' in others.

The trainees who responded to our survey suggested that a number of factors had caused them to have reservations about training to become teachers. The main things that 'put them off' teaching were:

- teachers' morale (17 per cent of respondents were moderately deterred and 4 per cent strongly deterred by this);
- salary (15 per cent moderately deterred, 5 per cent strongly deterred);
- how the public perceives teachers/teaching (12 per cent moderately deterred, 3 per cent strongly deterred);
- speaking to teachers about the profession (11 per cent moderately deterred, 3 per cent strongly deterred);
- spending more time in higher education (9 per cent moderately deterred, 3 per cent strongly deterred);
- TV drama programmes depicting the profession (7 per cent moderately deterred, 4 per cent strongly deterred).

Those student teachers whom we interviewed suggested that the two main considerations that had given them pause for thought were, first, the heavy workload that they associated with being a teacher and, second, issues relating to pupil behaviour and classroom management. Many of the student teachers we talked to spoke candidly about these issues, as illustrated in the following quotations:

> I think it was the workload . . . one of the things which made me say 'well, hang on, do I want this job to be my life or my career?' I think with teaching, I mean you know people say teaching shouldn't be your life, but it is really.
>
> (Male, 20–24, secondary)

All the teachers [I spoke to] were saying, 'oh dear, we were here [at school] until 7.30pm last night and we still haven't got all our work done.' I kept thinking [if I teach] I'm not going to have a life.

(Female, 20–24, primary)

Well, the one big one that I think everybody says, going into secondary [teaching], is the kids. The more you hear about it, the more you realise how terrible they are. I thought they were all going to be like animals.

(Male, 35–39, secondary)

A lot of the schools I was in when I was [an unqualified] supply teacher had pretty nasty kids where the teachers were off long term, so there were really negative interactions that you get to see . . . and how stroppy the kids can sometimes get . . . that was the main negative.

(Male, 25–29, secondary)

It is important to remember, however, that although some or all of these considerations may have deterred some potential teacher trainees from undertaking ITT and becoming teachers, those in our study who mentioned these concerns nevertheless had all still chosen to go for teaching. In fact, some of them talked about how they had chosen to undertake a teacher training programme in spite of their awareness of some of the drawbacks associated with teaching and suggested that, for them, the benefits of a career in teaching outweighed the costs:

You know, the huge personal commitment that you make to teaching. I mean that was part of the reason I stopped teaching English [abroad] for a while . . . And I had a break from it, and then after a while I really missed that because I felt like I wasn't doing anything that was meaningful.

(Female, 25–29, secondary)

Actually being a teacher obviously you get the worry, the discipline worries, and the behaviour issues, you know, that's fairly prominent just because of the stuff in the press and the legal responsibilities you've got, but . . . it didn't put me off in the slightest, I just fancied the challenge.

(Male, 20–24, primary)

You might thus say that these student teachers entered teacher training with their eyes wide open. Can you say you are making your decision with your eyes open? Are you confident that, with support and training, you will be able to deal with those issues that you perceive as drawbacks of being a teacher?

How confident are you that you will make an effective teacher?

Some people think that there is a universal 'checklist' of qualities, skills or knowledge that all effective teachers have, which you can measure your-selves against, and use to decide how suited you might be to teaching. It is true that all countries will have more or less explicit norms or standards. In England, a current understanding of what these qualities, skills and forms of knowledge might be is embodied in the present 'Standards for the Award of QTS' (Qualified Teacher Status), towards which student teachers will be working during their ITT. The current 'Standards' are organised into three sections:

1 *Professional values and practice*, e.g. 'they [teachers who meet the Standards] treat pupils consistently, with respect and consideration, and are concerned for their development as learners'; 'they are able to improve their own teaching, by evaluating it, learning from the effective practice of others and from evidence'.
2 *Knowledge and understanding*, e.g. 'they have a secure knowledge and understanding of the subject(s) they are trained to teach'; 'they understand how pupils' learning can be affected by their physical, intellectual, linguistic, social, cultural and emotional development'.
3 *Teaching*, with separate criteria relating to 'planning, expectations and targets', 'monitoring and assessment' and 'teaching and class management', e.g. 'they differentiate their teaching to meet the needs of pupils, including the more able and those with special educational needs'; 'they set high expectations for pupils' behaviour and establish a clear framework for classroom discipline'.

The full version of the Standards is available via the TDA website at www.tda.gov.uk/upload/resources/pdf/q/qualifying_to_teach.pdf.

There are both champions and critics of, and merits and demerits as-sociated with, the use of such Standards (or 'competences') to assess the capability of beginning (and other) teachers. If you decide to go for teacher training, you will eventually have to demonstrate that you 'measure up' against the Standards in order to complete your course successfully. So, any published 'standards' in your country can provide a useful insight into some aspects of what being a teacher entails and the expectations of your system. If, however, you want to decide whether you have what it takes to become a *student* teacher, and want to use any written standards to help you do so, do remember that there are many different possible starting points for journeys to a particular destination. In addition, because contexts (people, places and time) are constantly different, and because the research work into finding out and describing what does in fact constitute effective teaching is ongoing, even if standards are published they can still only be fairly general guidelines. But, and this is very useful, you have experience of the particular too! Teaching is the only profession of which everyone has such a vast experience of being 'on the receiving end', and this will have given you a wealth of knowledge about effective teachers and teaching from your own particular experience. So, as well as consulting any published standards, we suggest you think carefully of two or three teachers in your past that really helped you learn. Decide what kinds of attitudes, skills and knowledge they had. Which of these do you already possess? Has anyone ever told you 'you'd make a good teacher'? Have you ever helped someone learn something? If so, how did it make you feel?

Thinking about yourself, are you confident you could make a successful teacher? Can you explain to yourself why you think so? And would you be able to explain it to someone else in an interview for an ITT place?

The trainee whose words we quote below gave us, at the start of his one-year training, some of the reasons why he thought he would make a successful teacher:

> [A]s a person I'm quite outgoing, I'm quite . . . a confident person, and I think my communication skills are one of my strengths as are my . . . facilitation and group-working skills, and so really, yeah, I thought from quite an early age that I'd be . . . a candidate that would make a successful teacher.
>
> (Male, 20–24, secondary)

Your own experience of being a pupil and learner with many different teachers will doubtless also have taught you that there is more than one way of being a teacher and being an effective one. So what matters here is not that you can say exactly what the trainee we quote above said, but that you are confident that you, as a person, possess some of the skills, knowledge and enthusiasms that you associate (or your system associates) with being a good teacher, or that you associated with some of the effective teachers who have taught you.

Conclusion

In this chapter we have discussed a range of considerations that might attract you to or deter you from becoming a teacher, and we have raised a number of questions that might help you to decide whether you possess (or can develop) the qualities and skills necessary for becoming an effective teacher.

By now you should have a fairly clear idea rationally about whether teaching (and whether in primary or secondary schools) might be a good idea for you. However, for many, the moment of taking a decision is not, or not only, a rational process: feelings and intuition are also part of the 'thinking'. So, if by the end of reading this chapter you find that the logical process hasn't made your future clearer for you, or it does seem to be pointing you in one direction but 'something' (a feeling? your 'heart'?) is not convinced or even pulling you in the other direction, there is probably something you are still not yet taking into consideration – so read on! We are sure that by the time you reach the end of this book you will be able to make your decision, especially (for those of you who have not already done this) if you have also taken our advice to spend some time in different schools.

If you do choose to train to become a teacher, in most countries you will also be able to choose what type of ITT course you would prefer to follow and which ITT provider(s) you would prefer to be trained by. Issues relating to these choices are the subject of the next chapter.

Chapter 2

'It was the easiest and the quickest!'

Choosing an ITT route and provider

Introduction

Once you have decided (*if* you decide) that you want to train to become a teacher, most of you will then have more decisions to make. That is, in many countries prospective student teachers also have a choice about which of two or more broad types of ITT programme (or *routes* into teaching) they could follow, and in many countries you will have a further choice about which particular training provider or institution you would like to be trained by (and therefore apply to). In England there are (at the time of writing) over 200 providers of ITT courses and, though not all providers offer all ITT routes, prospective student teachers have a choice between a number of different broad types of ITT programme. The main ones, and those followed by the trainees in our research study, are listed below:

1 *University-administered Postgraduate Certificate in Education (PGCE) programmes*. These programmes typically last for one year and involve input from a higher education institution (HEI), and time spent in schools, which work in partnership with the HEI. More recently, Flexible PGCE programmes have been introduced, which contain the same training elements as a traditional PGCE programme but can be undertaken over a longer period of time.

2 *Undergraduate HEI-administered programmes*. These programmes lead to the award of a Bachelor of Arts (BA), Bachelor of Science (BSc) or Bachelor of Education (BEd) degree with Qualified Teacher Status (QTS). As with PGCE programmes, these degrees have input from both HEIs and partnership schools, although they typically last three or four years.

3 *School-centred Initial Teacher Training (SCITT) programmes*. These are normally organised and run by single schools or consortia of schools and typically last for one academic year. HEIs may or may not contribute to SCITT programmes, some of which are able to award a PGCE in addition to QTS.

4 *Graduate and Registered Teacher Programmes (GTP and RTP, collectively known as GRTP)*. These are employment-based routes into teaching. In both programmes student teachers are employed in a teaching post

whilst studying towards QTS. In the GTP student teachers already have a degree and (if successful) typically achieve QTS after the first year, whereas those undertaking the RTP complete their degree at the same time as undertaking teacher training and normally take around two years before being awarded QTS.

Other ITT routes that are available in England at this time are 'Teach First' (which was modelled on the US 'Teach for America' programme) and the Overseas Trained Teacher Programme (OTTP). More information about these routes is available on the website of the Training and Development Agency for Schools (TDA) at www.tda.gov.uk/Recruit/becomingateacher/waysintoteaching.aspx.

In the US, each state has its own initial teacher education requirements for those who wish to teach in public (i.e. state) school classrooms. When a 'probationer' meets these requirements a teaching certificate or licence is issued. The traditional route into teaching consists of a minor or major in education (depending on the age group a student teacher wishes to teach) at undergraduate level or a Master of Arts in Teaching. Alternative routes into teaching have, however, been developed, which again vary between states. It is therefore advisable to consult the education department of the state in which you wish to teach, although the National Council for Accreditation of Teacher Education (NCATE) is a useful first reference point (see www.ncate.org for further details). Likewise, teacher education in Australia is determined by individual state practice although training typically takes four years. Non-traditional routes (including employment-based routes) into teaching are offered in many countries, e.g. Germany, but they do not exist in countries such as Scotland, Japan and Korea.

In this chapter we discuss the kinds of questions it might be helpful to ask yourselves as you consider which kind of ITT route and which particular ITT provider(s) might be best for you. To help you think this through, we describe those issues that have actually impacted upon student teachers' choices of ITT route and provider. We begin by stressing the importance of doing your own research before making any decisions!

Do your own research

In order to even begin the decision-making process you need to arm yourself with relevant information about the routes available in your system. You will need to discover how many options there are and what the characteristics of each route are. For example, it is good to find out for each route:

- the duration of the programmes;
- whether the training takes place mainly or solely in schools or in some

other institution such as a university, or whether student teachers split their time between sites;
- whether successful completion of a programme via a particular route would provide you with 'qualified teacher status' only or also with some other qualification;
- whether different routes provide different kinds of financial support for the student teachers who follow them, or have other financial implications;
- what the entry requirements are and whether these differ from provider to provider;
- how many providers there are for each route and where these are geographically; and
- what percentages of student teachers who begin particular ITT routes with particular providers successfully complete their courses and go on to secure a teaching post.

What we are saying is that it is important that you make the right choice, and this needs to be an informed choice, and so we think it is wise, as a first step, to do your research carefully. Otherwise you might not actually get around to even considering an option that you *could* have decided was the best option *for you*. In fact, in our own research, we discovered that many people following ITT programmes in England had *not* been aware of the range of ITT routes that had been available to them. For example, only a quarter of all those trainees who were *not* following Graduate and Registered Teacher Programmes (GRTP) said that that they had known about these employment-based routes into teaching at the time they were applying for places on ITT programmes, while less than 35 per cent of respondents who were not following SCITT and flexible PGCE programmes indicated that they were aware of the existence of these routes. Those student teachers in our study who were aware of the choices available to them had consulted a range of sources of information, such as:

- people they knew who were following or had undertaken ITT courses themselves;
- the UCAS (Universities and College Admissions Service) website/ directory (this is the central body that processes admissions to all undergraduate and postgraduate HEI-based ITT programmes in the UK);
- the website of the Training and Development Agency for Schools (TDA), the national body responsible for the training and development of the school workforce, including teachers, teaching assistants and learning support workers (its website provides up-to-date information on the options available, the funding available for following different routes, and other related issues);

- the TDA information line (the TDA's telephone service designed to deal with queries relating to ITT);
- discussions with tutors/teachers working on the programme(s) they were considering;
- university/college or other ITT provider prospectuses;
- university/college or other provider websites;
- university/college or other provider 'open days'.

We also find that internet search engines such as Yahoo or Google can be a helpful means of finding out about this sort of information, and this may well lead you to some of the sources of information listed above.

Once you have armed yourself with all the information that you can find about your ITT route options and provider, the decision-making can begin! Some of you may at this stage be thinking that some routes are not in fact options for you – perhaps because you believe you don't have the entry requirements, or can't see how you could manage financially. For example, you may be a school-leaver and be tempted to discount postgraduate routes, or you may be a career-changer in England and assume that your only choice is a Flexible PGCE. We suggest you defer such decisions until you have thought through your responses to the remaining questions in this chapter, because if you discover that the route and provider that best suit *you*, as a person, are in fact ones that you might have discounted at this early stage, there may be ways you could get the extra qualifications you need, for example, or find the financial support for your preferred route. Consider the following questions:[1]

- How important is the *duration* of the training to you?
- How important are *financial considerations* to you?
- How important is the *nature and site* of the training to you? (For example, would you *prefer* to train and spend time in schools or universities or both? Do you think it would be *most beneficial* to you to train/spend most time in schools or universities or both? Do you think you would prefer or benefit most from a relatively 'practical' form of training or from training that included a relatively detailed emphasis on the 'theory' informing the practice?)
- How important is it to you where your training provider is geographically located?
- Are some ITT routes or providers held in higher regard than others and might these be more likely to help you to get a job on completion of your ITT?
- Is it important to you to train alongside other people who are also undertaking an ITT programme?
- Do your personal circumstances and/or existing commitments make some route options more viable than others?

- Are you pretty sure that you want to be a teacher or do you wish to keep your options open in some way (e.g. by taking a qualification that would be helpful for other career options too)?

In general, it is best to consider most seriously those factors that matter most to you – there are likely to be more than one, and they may be connected in different ways for different people. It is helpful to ask other people what mattered to them. And this is precisely what we have done in our research on your behalf. The student teachers in the 'Becoming a Teacher' study in England not only told us what factors influenced their choice of ITT route and particular provider, they also told us (at a later date) whether, if they had their time again, they would choose the same route and provider and if not, why not. Below we share the main findings with you and discuss some of the implications for the choices that you may need to make.

Choosing your ITT route

The student teachers who completed our questionnaire told us whether or not their choice of ITT route was influenced by one or more of 11 different considerations, and the main responses are presented in Table 2.1.

We can see that the most frequently given answer was that the *balance of course time spent in and out of schools* was an influential factor in their choice of route, and this is related to the third and ninth most frequently given responses – 'I wanted to be trained by qualified teachers in schools'

Table 2.1 Factors influencing student teachers' choice of ITT route (%)

The balance of in-school and out-of-school training appeals to me	46
I thought it was the best option financially	39
I wanted to be trained by qualified teachers in schools	35
I thought that prospective employers may prefer applicants who have followed this training route	34
I wanted to train alongside people in my peer group/in the same situation as me	34
It was available in my local area	32
It was available at the school/institution that I wanted to attend	26
I wanted to get a broader qualification before specializing in teaching	18
It was entirely school based rather than based in a university	12
The flexibility of the programme suits my other commitments	10

and 'it was entirely school based rather than based in a university.' The reasoning of some of the student teachers we talked to is illustrated in the following quotations. How important are any or all of these factors to you?

> I like the idea of the SCITT programme . . . because I thought . . . you learnt the theory but you learnt it through practice so you learn it and it underpins your practice . . . that I think was really important for teacher training that you actually work always in the context of the school environment, because it's very hard to get a feel or even an understanding of what a school environment is until you're actually in there.
>
> (Male, 20–24, secondary, SCITT)[2]

> I thought actually, at my stage in life, I don't really want to become a full time student . . . Because we're in a school, I can get a lot out of that environment because I've already worked for ten years and been in a work environment and can draw from other people, which I think comes from the experience of having worked already. So it was just, once I'd done my research, [the GTP route] looked like a much better way to do it for someone like me who's coming in as a career change.
>
> (Male, 30–34, primary, GTP)

> Partly I chose PGCE because my subject knowledge wasn't brilliant. I was concerned about that, and having sorts of gaps . . . I felt that I couldn't go into a secondary classroom having no experience of how to establish and maintain discipline, of classroom teaching, subject knowledge. Really, I felt that would be foolish in a way . . . [If I went straight] into a classroom and I was having to worry about discipline, how would I get classroom teaching and subject knowledge organised?
>
> (Female, 25–29, secondary, PGCE)

> I didn't want to [do a degree then a PGCE and] have to do everything in a year because I don't see, personally I don't think I would have been able to do it properly and be as I am now if I'd done three years of RE [my subject specialism] and then a teaching course. So I wanted to incorporate the two together.
>
> (Female, 20–24, secondary, BA QTS)

Three other factors were each mentioned by over a third of respondents as having been influential in their choice of ITT route: *financial considerations*; a wish to train alongside their *peers* or people in the 'same situation' as themselves; and a perception that *prospective employers* may prefer graduates from their chosen route. How important are these considerations to you?

Finance is a major issue for me because I already have my student loans and I didn't want to go down that route again . . . This [GTP route] is perfect really because it gives you that financial support but also you've only got a year and then hopefully you can look at getting a permanent job.

(Female, 20–24, primary)

I thought I could do [the Flexible PGCE] while I was still working and earning a living . . . My husband wasn't on a great wage at the time and I just thought 'I'm going to have to earn some money alongside doing this course'.

(Female, 25–29, primary)

What I thought the PGCE would do would be going through the training with a peer group, we were all going into the same pressures, the same things and in very much a team work environment.

(Female, 40–44, secondary)

I spoke to the head of my children's school. I didn't know whether to go down a [subject-specific degree] and then a PGCE [route]. But she said that she would take a BEd student over a PGCE student so I went down that route.

(Female, 30–34, primary)

The responses of some student teachers show that (other) practical or pragmatic considerations were also influential, with (for example) almost a third of student teachers saying that their choice of ITT route was influenced by its availability in their local area, and one in ten saying that the flexibility of their chosen route suited their other commitments. In addition, nearly one in five student teachers stated that they 'wanted to get a broader qualification before specializing in teaching' (were they keeping their options open or ensuring that they had something to fall back on in case teaching didn't work out?), whereas some of the student teachers we interviewed also talked about the importance to them of taking a 'vocational qualification'.

To be honest [I chose this route] because it was the nearest . . . I wanted to stay at home and I live locally so I could commute quite easily.

(Female, 20–24, secondary)

[With the Flexible PGCE] [y]ou can take a term out and you can come back and finish off that particular term with another group of students. That flexibility, especially with people like me, I have got young children you know. That gives me a huge breathing space, that I don't have to restart the whole academic year, but just do one more term, so that was the big plus point actually.

(Female, 40–44, primary)

[The SCITT programme I applied for] awards you the PGCE as well as the QTS and I think the PGCE is very important not only because it gives you the theoretical background which you work in, but also because I think it opens up a lot more doors in the future, maybe, not necessarily in teaching. So it's a very good qualification to have generically really.

(Male, 20–24, secondary)

I knew that when I came to university I wanted to do a degree where I'd have a job at the end of it, not just a general degree because I'm one of those people who I don't think would get motivated to do something after their degree. I wanted to have a degree so I'd have a job, I'd be trained in a profession at the end of it.

(Female, 20–24, secondary)

When we talked in detail to our student teacher interviewees, many of them (40 out of 85) said that there was another major influence on their choice of ITT route that we had not asked them about in the questionnaire. This related to *the length or duration of the ITT programmes* available to them, which was important in terms of both how long they wanted or felt able to devote to gaining a teaching qualification, and how much time they felt training to be a teacher would need and an ITT programme ought therefore to take. These two points are illustrated in the following quotations:

[I chose] PGCE because it was the easiest and quickest way to do the one year, basically a conversion degree.

(Female, 25–29, primary)

I want to be as good a teacher as I [can be], and . . . I'm doing it because I want to be a good teacher so you've got to do the four-year one to do it properly.

(Male, 20–24, primary)

One trainee, who had given up his job to train, linked course duration both to his age and to financial considerations:

I am not exactly super-old but I am coming up to 30. I didn't want to be, I didn't want three years of my life studying, it would have been too long. I am used to having a wage and a lifestyle.

(Male, 25–29, secondary)

Finally, Table 2.1 shows that as many as 26 per cent of our survey respondents said that their choice of ITT route was influenced by its availability at 'the school/institution that I wanted to attend' (i.e. at a particular *provider*). So what factors influenced our student teachers' (and might influence your) choice of ITT provider?

Choosing your ITT provider

As we can see in Table 2.2, two main considerations influenced the choice of ITT provider for the majority of student teachers who completed our questionnaire. The first was the *geographical location* of the provider, which 78 per cent of respondents said influenced their choice. Another 48 per cent and 14 per cent of respondents respectively gave the related answers 'I live in the local area/I could stay at home' and 'My partner lives/works/studies/ trains in the area.'

[To] be perfectly honest one of the things is geographical convenience . . . [The ITT providers I looked at] were close to where I lived and the schools that they covered were schools that I aspire to get a post at when I finish the course, so . . . I was quite selfish in that respect . . . if I could find a course that as well as providing me with the qualification I needed was close enough and convenient, that was an attraction, with

Table 2.2 Factors influencing student teachers' choice of ITT provider (%)

Geographical location of institution/school	78
Reputation of institution/programme	60
I live in the local area/I could stay at home	48
Good standard of schools in the local area	25
My partner lives/works/studies/trains in the area	14
I had previous experience of/in the school/institution	14
I know other people doing the programme	13
Reputation of particular trainers working on the programme	13
I know other people training at this school/institution	12

a family and everything. So that did influence the fact that I went for this course first.

(Male, 45 or over, secondary)

The second highest single response related to the *reputation* of the institution/programme, which 60 per cent of respondents said was influential, and another 13 per cent said that their choice was influenced by the 'reputation of particular trainers working on the programme.'

[I]t has got quite a good reputation and a couple of friends of mine have been here and trained here for the last three or four years as well.

(Female, 25–29, secondary)

[T]he fact that the [subject specialist is] . . . the local education authority subject person for all the schools in [county] gives you a huge advantage really because you're right up to date with everything. He's training all the other teachers so you feel like you're really involved with what's going on in the county and in the country as a whole in [subject specialism] . . . That was very attractive, you know, to know that you'd be receiving training from someone of that kind of calibre.

(Female, 25–29, secondary)

A quarter of respondents said that their choice of ITT provider was influenced by the *standard of schools* in the locality of the provider, which is likely to have related, for some trainees, to those concerns about pupil behaviour and classroom management that we discussed in Chapter 1 (and which we discuss further in Chapter 5). All of these factors are well worth considering.

Are you making the right choice?

In addition to the various issues discussed above, it might also be helpful, in deciding which ITT route and provider you are best suited to, to find out whether student teachers who had made similar decisions felt, after following their chosen route and programme, that they had made the right choice – and if not, why not.

When we asked 2,980 trainees who were just completing various kinds of ITT programmes in England whether, if they could go back in time, they would choose the same route and provider:

- just over three-quarters (76 per cent) said they would follow the *same route with the same ITT provider*;

- 8 per cent said they would follow the *same route but with a different provider*;
- 14 per cent said they would follow a *different ITT route*; and
- 2 per cent didn't know.

Those trainees who said they would choose a different ITT route were asked why. The main reasons were:

- 'I would want a route which provides a better balance of in-school and out-of-school training' (24 per cent);
- 'I would want a route which provides (more) financial assistance' (23 per cent);
- 'I would want a route with a more manageable workload' (22 per cent).

The first two explanations are now starting to sound familiar – they were two of the biggest influences on people's choice of ITT route in the first place, and these research findings reinforce their importance. The third explanation will be familiar from Chapter 1, where we showed that workload was perceived as one of the main 'deterrents' or drawbacks associated with becoming a teacher. The long and short of it is that many teachers find it difficult to achieve what they see as a satisfactory work–life balance, and student teachers find this especially hard . . . but you might find that some ITT routes fit with your personal circumstances better than others.[3]

With regard to the first point ('balance of in-school and out-of-school training'), most student teachers (apart from those following employment-based routes) tend to think that ITT programmes put too much emphasis on 'theoretical' issues (normally explored in universities) and too little emphasis on 'practical', school-based elements. But this issue is more complex than it appears, and is a point to which we return in Chapters 3 and 6. For now, we would want to caution you against writing off 'theory' – it can be practical and useful, and help you to become a better teacher too! So, while we hope that your thinking about your choice of ITT route and provider is becoming much clearer, we suggest you postpone any final decisions until you have read Chapters 3 and 6.

Conclusion

In this chapter we have raised a number of considerations that you might usefully think about before you come to a decision about which ITT route you would prefer to follow and which institution or providers you would prefer to be trained by (assuming that you first choose to undertake an ITT programme). Although we have suggested that you might postpone any final decisions until you have read some or all of the following chapters, we hope that your thinking about these issues – and your answers to the specific questions we raised at the start of the chapter – has developed.

In the next chapter we seek to encourage those of you who *are* going to train to become a teacher to uncover and develop your existing ideas about teaching and teacher training, with a view to helping you to make the most of (or get the most out of) your ITT.

'You build teachers up into these god-like people who are fantastic and amazing and how will you ever be that perfect?'

Preparing to make the most of your ITT

Introduction

Once you have made your decisions about training to becoming a teacher and about your preferred ITT route and provider, and once you have secured a place on an ITT programme, the next thing you need to do is to prepare *yourself* for starting your course. To do this you will need to use your imagination as well as some introspection, and this chapter supports you in doing that. Here, we ask you to think carefully about what you are looking forward to about your ITT course, what your expectations are, what concerns you have (if any), and what you think you need to learn as well as how you think you might learn it. As you read this chapter you will discover ways to get the most out of your ITT. Those of you who might still need to undergo some kind of selection interview before you are accepted onto a course will find this chapter helpful when preparing for that too.

On the other hand, if you have not yet made your decisions about whether or not to follow an ITT course and/or about which ITT route or provider(s) to apply to, reading this chapter might help you to make one or more of these decisions. That is, it will be helpful for you to find out about:

- what student teachers who had decided to go for a career in teaching were most looking forward to about their training;
- what they were most concerned about prior to starting their courses – bearing in mind that such concerns had not deterred them from choosing to follow an ITT course in the first place; and
- their expectations about what and how they would learn.

Having discussed each of these three important issues in turn, we end the chapter, and this first section of the book, by presenting some important advice offered by recently qualified teachers to those who are thinking about undertaking, or about to begin, an ITT programme.

What aspects of ITT are you looking forward to?

The student teachers in our research said that the main things they were looking forward to, before starting their ITT programmes, were:

- being in classrooms and interacting with pupils (mentioned by 84 per cent of survey respondents);
- developing an understanding of teaching and learning (73 per cent);
- learning to teach their specialist subjects (60 per cent);
- learning from practising teachers (58 per cent); and
- becoming part of a school community (45 per cent).

Are you looking forward to any of these things and/or to other things associated with undertaking an ITT course and (beyond this) becoming a teacher?

It makes sense that, if you are to enjoy teaching as a career, you'll need to enjoy being in classrooms, as this is where you'll spend most of your time! You'll also need to enjoy interacting with children (pupils) because this is what you'll spend large portions of your time doing. If you can't say you are looking forward to this aspect of your training, it may be because you have not yet taken up our suggestion in Chapter 1 to get some experience as an adult in schools. If you *have* taken this advice and are still not looking forward to spending time in classrooms, it might be useful to reflect once more on why you want to undertake an ITT course and whether you are making the right career decision. It may be, on the other hand, that you feel that you *will* be able to look forward to this aspect of being a teacher once you have overcome one or more of any *concerns* you may have about teaching in general or this aspect of teaching in particular (which we discuss later in the chapter). This is quite common and perfectly natural.

In order to enjoy and get the most out of an ITT course you will also need to enjoy learning of various kinds. As one of the student teachers one of us taught once said (although unfortunately at the *end* of her programme): 'at first I thought this programme was about my teaching, now I know it was about my learning'. Many people starting out on ITT programmes think that it is all about *their teaching*. In one sense of course this is so, but it is actually more helpful to think about an ITT course as being primarily concerned with your learning (of teaching and being a teacher). The learning you will need to do includes:

- developing a *pedagogical* view of your 'subject' (or, if you already have one, subjecting this to critique and further development);
- developing informed planning skills (informed by an understanding of how the subjects you teach can be learnt, by knowledge of a range of strategies that could be used to support that learning, knowledge of a whole range of contextual issues, and much more);
- developing the ability to use strategies skilfully in particular classrooms with particular learners to support their learning;
- developing the ability to assess that learning as well as your own work; and
- developing professional ways of being, thinking and acting that are appropriate to your context.

And that was a very brief summary! We say this not to put you off, but rather to suggest that if you are not looking forward to learning you may need to think carefully about whether undertaking an ITT programme or being a teacher is for you. (And how will you be able to instil a love of learning in pupils if you don't have it yourself?) Having said that, we believe that the 'learning instinct' is an inherently human thing (just think of how much babies and children learn before they even arrive in official 'learning places' – schools), and we know from research (Csikszentmihalyi, 1990) that most adults derive satisfaction from engaging in new challenges. This might explain why those who do love teaching do so in part for the continuous opportunities for learning that it brings.

From thinking about what you might be looking forward to, we turn now to thinking about what might be worrying you when you think about following an ITT course.

What are you concerned about?

Forewarned is forearmed, as they say, so it makes sense in this phase of preparing yourself to get the most out of your ITT programme to face your concerns and assess as far as you can whether they are justified, and, if so, to consider what you could do *now* to address them. Before you read on, make a note somewhere of any concerns you have about doing an ITT course.

The student teachers in our study were asked in a questionnaire to say whether before starting their ITT they had any concerns or worries about the course. Three issues were each identified as concerns by over half of the trainees. These were:

- whether they would be able to manage the workload (69 per cent);
- whether they would be able to maintain discipline in the classroom (66 per cent);
- whether they would be able to manage financially (53 per cent).

These concerns were similar to trainees' views about the main drawbacks to teaching as a career, which we discussed in Chapter 1. Are your concerns similar? If they are, the discussion below may help you. If they were different, you may find that the way we now discuss the concerns listed above (and additional concerns described below) will help you to address yours.

Regarding the biggest of the three concerns listed above, different routes into teaching may be more or less intensive, and programmes in different systems will have different requirements in terms of assessments, such as the number of essays to write, portfolios to construct or complete, lessons to teach and plans to produce. Yet you can be sure that they have one thing in common – they will *all* require quite a lot of work, partly because, as we pointed out above, there is a lot to learn. It will be important to keep focused and deal with work as it arises. As one of the trainees in our research advises:

> Once you start training be ready for it to be challenging and just keep focused on doing things as they come up rather than panicking about the volume of the workload.
>
> (Female, 25–29, secondary)

It is also a good idea if you can to speak to recent graduates of the programme you are considering or about to start, in addition to consulting programme documentation, to get as clear an overall picture as you can about the work that you will need to do, when you will need to do it, and how much time the different tasks are likely to take you. And unless you are very good at time management and at estimating how long things will take to complete, it is worth remembering the old advice of thinking of a time-span, doubling it, then doubling it again! But remember that, although it is hard, it is all 'doable' – the statistics show that every year the majority of student teachers successfully complete their programmes.

A second reason why you may not be looking forward to being in classrooms and interacting with pupils could be to do with concerns over the necessity for dealing with *pupil behaviour* of various sorts and your ability to manage this aspect of the work. We saw above that two-thirds of the student teachers in our study (all of whom had already made the decision to begin an ITT course) said that they had such concerns, so it would be natural for you to have similar worries. But although in many parts of the world pupil behaviour in classrooms is certainly an issue, it is important to be aware that the teachers and tutors associated with your chosen ITT programme will support you in thinking through and developing skills in employing contextually appropriate strategies for managing pupil behaviour (and learning!). We also discuss behaviour management strategies ourselves in Chapter 5 of this 'course companion'.

As for the third concern listed above, *financial worries*, our best advice here would again be to do your research carefully about routes that might best suit your financial circumstances, and to look carefully and realistically at your financial needs. If you do then make a rational decision that it would be financially feasible to undertake ITT, decide what that will mean for you in terms of realistic budgeting and perhaps practise living within that budget for a while. In our experience, the thought of having to adapt to changed financial circumstances, for example, is often more worrying than the reality. Anything you can do to help yourself allay these worries now will give you more time and focused energy to devote to your studies when you begin your course.

In addition to the three main concerns above, many of the trainees in our study said they had a number of specific concerns which related to (1) wanting to be successful on their courses; (2) wanting to be successful teachers; and (3) remaining doubts about their initial decisions.

1   Being successful on their ITT course:
  •   whether they 'would be able to cope with the academic difficulty of the course' (49 per cent);
  •   whether they would 'be able to pass the skills tests' (35 per cent);[1]
  •   whether they 'would get sufficient help for teaching' (32 per cent).

2   Being successful as a teacher:
  •   whether they 'would be able to bring about pupil learning' (46 per cent);
  •   whether they 'would be able to develop rapport with the children I teach' (27 per cent);
  •   whether they 'would get along with teachers and other staff in school' (24 per cent); and
  •   whether they 'would be able to deal with pastoral issues' (12 per cent).

3   Remaining doubts about their initial decisions:
  •   whether they 'would enjoy the teaching/training' (37 per cent).

1 Being successful on your ITT course

With regard to the first of these three groups of concerns, it is natural to be a little concerned about whether you will in fact be able to match up to expectations and *be successful on your course*. After all, this is something you haven't done before and so you have not yet proved to yourself that you can do it. However, remembering two things may help to allay these concerns at this stage. First of all, you have had many successes in the past – in obtaining the qualifications that enable you to even consider teacher training, for example. Second, it should help to know, if you have been or are accepted onto a course, that experienced teacher educators associated with the course believe you can be successful. With regard to concerns about whether or not you will get sufficient help, it might be useful to remember that you will have an important part to play in this. Your whole course will be structured to help you, but teacher educators will be busy and (often) involved with many trainees, and they are not (even if they sometimes seem to be!) mind-readers. So if you need help you may need to ask for it. You will also need to remember that 'help' can come from many sources – your coursemates, books, your family members and teachers in schools (whether they are your official 'mentor' or not).

2 Being successful as a teacher

Looking at those concerns relating to being successful as a teacher, we think the first one is a good one to have at the beginning of your course, as 'being able to bring about pupil learning' is the core of the business of teaching and the main focus of what you will need to learn! Having said that, it should help to remember that the main aim of your ITT course is to help you to learn skills that will enable you to bring about pupil learning – even if it isn't always obvious to you how some aspects of your course are relevant to this goal. We might add that concerns relating to bringing about pupil learning may well continue to preoccupy you throughout your career, as, although we can all get better over time at enabling learning to happen for more of our learners more of the time, we doubt that there is one teacher who enables learning to happen for *all* of their pupils/'learners' *all* of the time. Now, on the one hand, this might seem a bit alarming if you expected by the end of your ITT to be able to help *all* your pupils learn *all* of the time. On the other hand, it is this constant challenge that is one of the reasons why many find teaching an endlessly rewarding and fascinating career.

The other concerns relating to being successful as a teacher also suggest that the student teachers in our study were aware of the centrally important role of interpersonal relationships in this career. This is a theme we shall return to on many occasions in this book (and in Chapter 7 in particular), but for now, if you share these concerns, there may be ways you can start to allay them. For example, if you are concerned about your ability to develop a rapport with your pupils, you might consider finding and spending (more) time with children of the age group you are intending to teach. This will help you begin to discover general characteristics of the age group, such as how they see the world and the kinds of things they are interested in and motivated by. In other words, you can deepen your understanding of them, which is the key to developing a good rapport. Of course, you will still need to listen to and observe carefully the particular children you teach, but preparing yourself by gaining more familiarity with the age group will be a good start.

Good, trusting relationships with other adults in school are indeed also very important, particularly (during your ITT) those with your mentor. We discuss ways of managing difficulties in such relationships, should they arise, in Chapter 7. Here, it is perhaps appropriate to remind you of what your experience will have taught you about what it takes to start and build a trusting relationship. For example, it requires *time* and it is *two-way*. That is, it requires both partners to get to know each other and a willingness on both sides to spend time together, communicate with each other and 'self-disclose' (or reveal personal information). So, for example, you will probably expect your mentor to make efforts to get to know and understand you, but don't forget that you will need to try to get to know and understand your mentor too.

3 Remaining doubts

Will you enjoy ITT and teaching?

Finally, some student teachers who filled in our questionnaire were still wondering if they would enjoy their ITT. We hope that if you have thought carefully about the issues we raise in this chapter, and indeed the whole book, you will be well prepared to *make the most of* your ITT and will have a good/better idea about whether or not you are likely to enjoy ITT and teaching. However, on the question of whether you will *actually* enjoy ITT and teaching, the proof of the pudding will ultimately be in the eating. We wish you luck but would add that you sometimes 'make your own luck'! We suggest that you always try to retain a sense of perspective and to remember the specific aspects of teaching you do enjoy and look forward to, rather than focus on the things which may not be going so well. You may be tempted to focus on the negative if (for example) you have an overly critical (for you) mentor *and/or* are a perfectionist *and/or* are keen or expect to learn more quickly than you are doing *and/or* are 'Eeyore-ish' in character[2] and find gloom appealing! But if you find yourself tempted into overly negative ways of thinking for whatever reason, the old advice to 'count your blessings' and list what is going right for you could help maintain perspective!

Developing a teacher identity

When we talked at length to some of the student teachers in our study, some of them mentioned a different kind of concern about which we hadn't asked the larger group who took part in the survey. This concern was about the general idea of becoming and *feeling like a teacher*, or taking on the *identity* of a teacher. For example, some of those entering ITT straight from

A-level courses or undergraduate courses, or with little break in between to pursue alternative careers, talked about concerns relating to the transition to a professional lifestyle and the responsibilities associated with this.

> It always seemed like very sort of high status, you know. A lot of responsibility. You have to be very knowledgeable, know everything really! . . . [B]ecause you build, when you want to be a teacher, you build teachers up into these god-like people who are fantastic and amazing and how will you ever be that perfect?
>
> (Female, 20–24, primary)

If one of the concerns you noted earlier seems connected to this theme (or if you think it is a concern now that we have mentioned it!), it might help you at this stage to remember two or three good teachers you have had. Although they may have had some characteristics in common, we are sure you can think of things they said or did, or mannerisms they had, or particular ways of dressing, or personal interests they told you about, that will remind you that they were all very different people and perhaps different 'types' of teacher. In other words, different kinds of people can and do become teachers, and remain *themselves* at the same time. And all 'teachers' were once like you – that is, 'not teachers'!

In our research, it was not only the people who had not yet entered the world of work who were concerned about developing a *teacher identity*. Some of those who had previously worked in schools in various support roles (e.g. as 'teaching assistants') reported a number of concerns about the transition from working *for* a teacher to actually *being* a teacher. For example, some trainees expected that, should they train in the same school, they would be viewed by staff, pupils and/or parents as still in their old role, and this might undermine their ability to develop as teachers. The solution for some was to try to ensure that they could move school to avoid this scenario, and make a 'fresh start'. Nevertheless, some of those who remained in or found themselves in the same school saw these prior concerns as 'false fears', as suggested in the quotation below, and we would add that there are also advantages in being in familiar surroundings (e.g. with fewer changes to adapt to there is more 'headspace' for the new challenges of ITT).

> I was a bit concerned because having been a support assistant [the pupils] always knew that I wasn't the one in charge, the teacher was and ultimately had the final word. So I was a bit worried that when I started teaching they wouldn't look at me like that, but I've not had any problems at all with that. They seem to have accepted the fact that I'm a teacher now and I tell them what to do and they do it. It's been all right.
>
> (Female, 30–34, secondary)

What do you need to learn during ITT?

We have already said a little about the kinds of things people becoming teachers need to learn, but here, and in preparation for getting the most out of your ITT, we want you to think about what you feel, at this stage, that *you* most need to learn. Again, it might be helpful to make a few notes about your immediate thoughts before reading on.

In our questionnaire, student teachers were asked how important they had thought it was (before they started their ITT) that they should develop each of 14 different kinds of knowledge or skill. The highest numbers of respondents stated that it was very important for student teachers to develop what we might call 'practically oriented classroom-based outcomes':

- 91 per cent said they had thought that it was very important that trainees learn the 'ability to bring about pupil learning';
- 86 per cent thought it very important that trainees should learn the 'ability to maintain discipline in the classroom'; and
- 74 per cent stated that they considered it very important that they develop 'knowledge about their teaching subjects'.

All of these ideas are related to in-class behaviour and suggest that most of the student teachers in our survey were imagining themselves as teachers in classrooms, and wanting to bring about learning through their teaching, whilst recognising that a pre-condition for this is good classroom management. (*Were/are your ideas similar?*) As people who have been pupils and students watching and experiencing the work of teachers for years, it is understandable that you might think you already know about all or most of what you have to learn because you are so familiar with what teachers do in classrooms. But there is a lot more to being a teacher than what pupils see, and we could liken a teacher to an iceberg – with the much smaller visible tip being the observable in-class behaviours of teachers and demonstrations of subject knowledge or expertise, and the greater important mass remaining unseen. Or, as one of our case study trainees reported her lecturer as saying, 'being a teacher is like being a swan: elegant and refined on top and paddling like mad under the water.' In other words there is a *lot* going on underneath or 'back-stage'.

Quite a large group (over 70 per cent) of the student teachers who answered our questionnaire realised they would need to learn some 'invisible' things, and stated, for example, that they had believed that it was very important that student teachers develop:

- 'knowledge/understanding of pupil motivation and behaviour' (73 per cent); and
- 'how pupils learn' (71 per cent).

But fewer trainees thought it was 'very important' for them to develop (for example):

- the 'ability to deal with pastoral issues' (35 per cent);
- an awareness of 'research findings about effective teaching methods' (23 per cent);
- 'knowledge/understanding of the philosophy of education' (10 per cent); and
- 'knowledge/understanding of the history of education' (5 per cent).

The point is that many student teachers enter ITT expecting that the ITT course content will have 'theoretical' parts and 'practical' parts, and they don't care as much for the former! That some trainees think in this way is quite understandable, for a number of reasons. First, being novices (when it comes to facilitating learning), most trainees see or recognise only the 'tip of the iceberg' or the elegance of the gliding swan. Second, it is natural to be more concerned, when you first start training to be a teacher, about 'practical' issues, such as behaviour management and wanting to be accepted as a teacher by more established members of the profession, than about those aspects of course provision that may seem less directly related to the 'front-stage' work of the teacher. And all adults (in particular) are concerned that what they spend their valuable time learning should be relevant to the purposes they have in mind. However, although it is understandable for trainees to have little interest in the 'theoretical' elements of ITT course provision, this can also hold you back in your development as a teacher. So how might we help you to see things differently?

Let's start from the point that ITT course designers and teacher educators have good reasons for including these more 'theoretical' aspects in your course – if you can't see how or why they are useful, just ask! Again, we'll come back to this issue in Chapter 6, but for now it might give you a head start if we explain a little what we mean. We think there are two main ways in which 'theories' are in fact practical and useful both for in-class 'paddling' and for the unseen (to pupils) work of teachers outside classrooms. The first way is to see 'theories' as possible *explanations* of events that occur in classrooms, because finding the best 'explanation' (there is rarely only one possible explanation) may be the key to working out the most appropriate thing to do next. Much of an expert teacher's in-class 'paddling' has to do with noticing what is happening and thinking – almost instantaneously and more or less consciously – about various explanations of those events to make on-the-spot decisions about what to say or do next. In order to help you reach that stage in the medium or longer term you need, in the short term (during your ITT), to learn about the various possible ways of explaining things and to practise using them when thinking about and discussing things you have heard and seen in schools and classrooms.

The other way in which 'theories' are useful is as *tools*, which are practically helpful in planning and reviewing teaching. 'Theories' about how your subject is learnt, for example, will usually suggest sequences of activities to support that learning process, and this can serve as a kind of checklist to help in lesson-planning or in helping you to work out why pupils don't always learn as much as you had expected or hoped.

Although a number of rather different things counted as 'theory' for the trainees in our study, and we discuss this more fully in Chapter 6, if you can start your course with this suggested way of seeing those parts of your course which are less obviously and directly connected with in-class teaching, it will be helpful to your learning and your teaching.

How valuable do you expect different learning strategies in ITT to be?

It might help you get the most out of your course to think about not only what you will be learning but how you will learn it. What do you think now will be the most valuable aspects of your course? What kinds of things are you expecting to be asked to do to support your learning?

In our questionnaire we also asked student teachers how important or unimportant they thought it was, before they started their ITT, that their ITT programme should include different teaching and learning strategies. Again our findings suggest that a large proportion of trainees started their ITT with a focus on the need to learn mainly the visible aspects of teaching. The highest number of respondents stated they had considered it to be very important to:

- have 'school teachers/mentors observe your lessons and give feedback' (75 per cent);
- 'watch schoolteachers teach' (74 per cent);
- get 'assistance with lesson planning' (71 per cent);
- be 'given specific strategies for teaching specific subjects/topics' (66 per cent).

In contrast:

- a relatively low 48 per cent of respondents indicated that they had considered it very important to 'study ideas about how pupils learn'; and
- only 22 per cent of respondents stated that they had thought that it was very important to study 'current research on teaching methods'.

If you had similar ideas, we hope we may have begun to help you see how *all* aspects of what you are asked to learn and how your course is designed are there for very good and *practical* reasons.

Tips from recently qualified teachers

We end this chapter, and the first section of the book, by presenting the main responses given by second-year teachers (most of whom had successfully completed both their ITT and their NQT (Newly Qualified Teacher) Induction programmes in England) to the following question:

> If you could give one piece of advice to someone considering becoming a teacher, what would it be?

As well as providing further food for thought about how you might make the most of your ITT course, these 'tips' might also help those of you still undecided about whether to train to be a teacher to make your decision. On this (last) matter, one or two of our research participants said things such as:

> My instant response would be 'don't do it'! But lots of people said that to me and I didn't listen!
>
> (Female, 30–34, primary)

Another recently qualified teacher, on the other hand, said:

> The only piece of advice to anyone wanting to become a teacher I would give is to do it; kids aren't as bad as they're often made out to be and the satisfaction and rewards I have experienced right from the start of my training far outweigh the occasional bad day.
>
> (Male, 35–39, secondary)

These different views suggest that it really is a question of whether teaching suits *you*, as the advice from this teacher (and some others who we quote below) makes clear:

> My advice to people considering a career as a teacher would be to think about their characters and whether they would be really happy with the practical and personal aspects of being a teacher.
>
> (Female, 25–29, primary)

We have organised the other helpful tips into eight main themes.[3]

1 Get some life experience first (or too)

> Get some life experience first!!!! I feel this job is much easier to handle

if you are able to look on the task more objectively and have some other keen interest in your life with which to balance the teaching job!

(Female, 40–44, secondary)

2 Decide if it suits you

Check carefully that you understand what it involves, pros and cons. Ask some good friends if they think you would be a good teacher and what age range would suit your personality.

(Male, 30–34, primary)

Experience it beforehand, try out various ages and schools before you commit.

(Female, 20–24, primary)

I am too much of an introverted, intellectual and complicated character, in many ways, to be a primary teacher, at least in a standard and not especially easy, state school. I was beginning to figure out effective classroom management techniques, and learning how to project the right image, but it didn't come naturally and I didn't like having to behave like a certain kind of teacher. If I reacted to the children and to things that happened naturally, I was not able to maintain order effectively and teaching became impossible. I could see that it was going to be a very uphill struggle and it was making me unhappy.

(Female, 25–29, primary)

Be sure that you can afford to live on the wages!

(Male, 45 or over, secondary)

3 Be realistic – it's hard work

Ensure you are going into teaching for the right reasons – don't look upon it as an easy option because it isn't, forget the idea of 9 till 3 etc. that the public perceive.

(Female, 20–24, primary)

Expect to be tired and spend a lot of what should be free time, making resources, marking etc.

(Female, 40–44, secondary)

It's worth a try but a career will be difficult unless you are unbelievably dedicated and want to work long hours.

(Female, 20–24, secondary)

4 . . . but rewarding

I would still tell people that teaching is rewarding and extremely hard work.

(Female, 35–39, primary)

Go for it! Ignore the older and cynical teachers, it is a fantastic job! [It is] [h]ard work crippled with paperwork but the kids are great!

(Female, 30–34, secondary)

5 . . . with highs as well as lows

Teaching is one of the best jobs in the world. It has its highs as well as lows. Not every day can be the best one and try to remember that when it is your low point.

(Female, 25–29, primary)

6 Remain calm

To stay calm . . . teaching is like being a swan, elegant and refined on top and paddling like mad under the water.

(Female, 20–24, primary)

7 About the pupils/learners

Always remember that you do not know what happens to your students outside school hours and take account of this when making judgments about them.

(Female, 45 or over, secondary)

Treat the pupils as equals – they respond better that way.

(Male, 20–24, secondary)

8 Be organised and manage your time and workload

Make sure when you get a job that you try to balance your home and work life and don't work too hard.

(Female, 20–24, primary)

Apart from 'you must be mad!' I would say get organised, find a system that works for you and go with it. And don't worry about the stuff that doesn't get done, the world won't end if you don't mark the books instantly!

(Female, 20–24, primary)

I would tell someone thinking of becoming a teacher that the job is very rewarding but the key to still having a social life is being very organised. I make use of every free lesson to mark or prepare resources and this means that I have to take very little marking home. Home is just for planning lessons. It is too easy to get sidetracked during 'frees' and end up chatting but the resulting stress I have decided is not worth it! Leave socialising in the staff room for break and lunchtime!

(Female, 25–29, secondary)

Conclusion

In this chapter we have sought to prepare those readers who have made the decision to undertake an ITT programme to make the most of that programme, while also seeking to help those people who have not yet decided to make their decision. We hope both groups of readers have found this helpful.

We begin Section 2 of the book by discussing student teachers' early experiences of ITT and of becoming a student teacher, and suggest ways of dealing with the emotional roller-coaster that this frequently involves.

Section 2

Being a student teacher

Chapter 4

'It's all a bit overwhelming at first!'

Dealing with the emotional roller-coaster of beginning a teacher training course

Introduction

Has your introduction to ITT and schools had its ups and downs? Are you feeling overwhelmed or emotionally drained by your early experiences of ITT? If you are, you might take some comfort from the fact that, according to our research (and in our experience):

- this is a common reaction amongst trainees; and
- the vast majority of trainees nevertheless go on not only to survive but eventually to thrive!

The beginning of your ITT programme is likely to be a busy and quite demanding time. In our research we found that trainees following different kinds of ITT route and programme experienced broadly similar early introductions to teaching in their ITT placement schools, in terms of activities undertaken. These included:

- getting to know the school environment and community – for example, by talking to heads of department and subject and Special Educational Needs (SEN) co-ordinators, and by reading school policies;
- observing experienced teachers teaching and pupils working; and
- working with class teachers to plan and teach or team-teach parts of lessons; before
- teaching whole lessons to full classes by themselves, normally under the observation of mentors or other teachers.

When they talked about their early experiences of their ITT programme, especially their early experiences in their first placement schools, many student teachers in our research said they felt they had been on an emotional roller-coaster. The high points and low points that they experienced were often related to their relationships with, and the behaviour towards them of, 'significant' other people including pupils, their mentors and other teachers in their placement schools. Just the very act of standing at the front of a class – and the responsibility that they associated with this – can be a shock to the system, as the student teacher quoted below illustrates:

> I'd done presentations at work [in my previous job] but still, standing in front of that number of people is a shocker . . . Nothing can prepare you for standing in front of the little so-and-sos!
>
> (Male, 30–34, secondary)

The 'highs' and 'lows' experienced by student teachers are often also related to the fact that, in many contexts, the trainees are operating in a 'high-pressure' environment in which their mentors and/or others must assess them against a set of 'standards' for achieving Qualified Teacher Status (QTS). Trainees are thus conscious that if they are not judged to meet the Standards, they will not pass their ITT course. And this can encourage them (and you) to behave in ways which aren't conducive to learning to become a teacher. We come back to this point later. In this chapter we discuss:

- some of the common sources of worry, frustration and unhappiness that those beginning an ITT course might encounter;
- some of the strategies that have been – and might be – employed for dealing with 'lows' in general and with specific lows in particular; and
- some of the positives that people have taken – and you might take – from their/your experiences of ITT.

Are your early experiences of ITT proving difficult or frustrating, or making you unhappy?

Before you read on about the sources of frustration or unhappiness for the trainees in our research, you might need to know that later in this chapter (and in the book) we suggest strategies for dealing with these situations and feelings. In other words our intention is not to put you off, or increase your worries, but rather to help you get both a realistic picture and perhaps a sense of relief from the fact that any worries or difficulties you may experience or be experiencing are not unusual for novice teachers.

Trainees we spoke to told us of difficulties and stresses associated with different aspects of the design and implementation of the programme they were following, with developing and maintaining productive relationships with people in schools, and with the impact on their family lives of following an ITT programme. More specifically, the early difficulties most frequently encountered (in the order we present them here) related to:

- achieving a work–life balance;
- the period of school-based observation prior to teaching;
- difficulties in making the transition to a teacher role;
- difficult relationships with mentors and other school teacher colleagues;

- difficult relationships with, and difficulties caused by the behaviour of, pupils/students; and
- a perceived overemphasis on 'theory'.

We discuss each of these difficulties (or sources of frustration or unhappiness) in turn, and offer some guidance or strategies for dealing with each.

I The impact of undertaking ITT on your family/ social/non-work life

In most parts of the world your ITT programme will require a considerable commitment of time and effort, which may, temporarily at least, impact on your home or family life. One of our older career-changer research participants explained:

> [I]t is hard because if I am honest I have probably given teacher training more than I have given my family . . . which is why there is the guilt. The guilt possibly does affect [me] at times, but if I am honest, I am that determined to actually do this that I have put it ahead of my family.
>
> (Female, 35–39, primary)

So what are your circumstances? Have you obtained the support of those closest to you and explained that you may, for the duration of the ITT course at least, be less available to them than you once were or ideally would be? Alternatively (or in addition) can you work on becoming more organised and managing/using your time more effectively? Here's a story that may help you think about this:

> A man took a large jar and filled it with rocks. He asked those standing near him whether it was full. 'Yes' they said, 'because no more rocks will go in it.' The man took some pebbles, and put them into the jar and they fell down through the spaces between the rocks. 'Oh!' gasped the bystanders. 'Is it full now?' asked the man. Most bystanders said 'yes', but a few said 'maybe not'. The man then took a bag of sand, and poured most of it into the jar in the small spaces between the rocks and the pebbles until the jar was full. 'You see!' said the few bystanders. 'Oh' gasped the others. The man asked again 'Is the jar full?' 'Well, now it must be' said most bystanders. 'Ummm' hesitated others. Then the man took a jug of water and poured most of that in too. 'What can this teach us about using our time?' asked the man. 'You can always fit more in' said one of the bystanders. The man replied, 'well that may be partly true, but more importantly it matters how we fill the jar of time.

If we fill the jar with sand, there will be no room for rocks or pebbles: we have to put the big rocks in first.'

When we are very busy, we find it helps to think of the tasks for the day or week as 'big rocks' (or larger tasks that are absolute priorities and need to 'go in first'), pebbles as smaller but quite urgent tasks (which can fit around these), and sand and water tasks that can be slotted in when there's a gap. Certain types of task can often be labelled as rock, pebble, sand or water, we find. For one of us (Angi!), for example, reading and responding to emails has on occasion easily filled the jar of the day with sand and left no room for the 'big rock' of writing another chapter of this book! So, it might help you to think of all the tasks for the week that you would ideally like to fit in (including those for your ITT and for your family) and, remembering the story above, make a plan accordingly.

2 Difficulties relating to undertaking a period of observation before teaching in schools

Many ITT programmes in many education systems now include a phase of observing in schools and classrooms as a lead-in to actual teaching experience. This period of observing followed by increasing amounts of teaching can occur at different stages of the actual programme. (In England, this observation phase usually either starts the programme or is provided very early on.) There are good reasons for preceding teaching by a phase of observation in schools, but not all the student teachers we spoke to seemed to have found this time valuable. For example, some of the student teachers in our research reported that they had found this initial observation phase to be monotonous and/or frustrating – and would have preferred to have been 'thrown in at the deep end' and 'left alone to get on with it'.

Imagine how boring it was, over those three weeks [an early observation phase in schools]. It was awful, it really was. You were under people's feet . . . I mean, even if you are helping in a class, you can only help so much. I think it was just to make sure people didn't hate schools.

(Female, 30–34, secondary)

As the trainee above suggests, one reason for an early experience observing in a school can be to allow trainees a final check on their decision to become a teacher. So, especially if you have had limited time in schools before starting your programme, you might like to ask yourself if you would be happy spending large parts of your time over the coming years in a school environment. However, do remember that not all schools are the same, and you could usefully start identifying what it is about the particular school you are in for your observation phase that you like or dislike, perhaps with a view to creating a checklist to use when you go for interviews for your first post (see Chapter 9).

However, there are several more important reasons related to teacher learning for why it will be helpful for your teaching for you to spend time observing. Most programmes will explain these to you and give you tasks to help you make the most of your time. But in case yours didn't, or you missed those sessions (or were distracted when they were explained, or suffering from information overload!), we'll suggest two main reasons here as well as some tasks you might like to try to help you learn from the experience.

Developing noticing skills

'A teacher's responsibility is his/her response-ability': a teacher's ability to respond to learning needs of pupils is fundamental to expert teaching, and this is based on *noticing* a myriad of small signs of learning or lack of attention or impending chaos or loss of class control. When you start teaching you will probably be so busy paying attention to what *you* want to say, your timing, your materials and how you do things that, until these become more automatic, you may have little space to notice the all-important tiny signals your pupils are sending you. So, this observation period is a useful time to:

a   try to spot what the teacher might have noticed that prompts him or her to say or do unplanned things (and the apparent effect of these); and

b   develop your own noticing skills.

For (a) above, for example, you could observe some teaching and make a note of all the instances when the teacher says or does something for which you did not spot the trigger. Then, as soon as possible after the lesson, ask the teacher what it was that they noticed that caused them to say or do the things you have noted (but don't be surprised if the teacher has some difficulty answering, as for him or her the 'noticing and responding' itself may well have become somewhat automatic). In subsequent lessons you could then try to spot the triggers before the teacher responds. Or you could see if different teachers respond to different types of triggers and try to work out why. What kinds of things do you imagine you would want to respond to, and why? You can use some of the time during your observation period to begin to develop a list of student behaviours that, if you saw or heard them in your classroom, you would want to respond to. This work can really help you later to spot such signals.

For (b) above, you could keep a 'noticing journal' (trying to take the perspective of the teacher) and, once a day in this observation phase, record (describe) what you noticed in a lesson. At the end of a week, look back over these descriptions and ask yourself what kinds of things you seem to be noticing (and not noticing) and why. Are you mainly describing what the teacher does or says, or what pupils do or say, what the boys (and not the girls, or vice versa) do or what a particular pupil does, or ways learning is supported, or ways classroom control is maintained, or the layout of the classroom and how this is used, or the tasks and materials that are used, or the forms of interaction in the classroom . . . ? And there are many many more things that could be noticed and that it is useful for teachers to think about. It might help to swap noticing journals with fellow trainees to compare the kinds of things you notice and to help you notice more. It is quite difficult to notice in familiar surroundings and, for us all, schools (because we have attended them for so long) are familiar places in many ways, so just finding out the kinds of things that others are noticing can help us notice more.

Observation to develop teaching skills

In learning any skill it is helpful to observe experts in action, so that we can pay attention to the main features and steps involved in their actions. These experiences can then act as templates or models for our own later first attempts. So, you can use the observation period to specifically observe aspects of teachers' practice and make notes on these. You might decide, for example, to choose a focus and look carefully at the ways different teachers manage their classes, or use whole-class or group work, or employ a particular subject-specific pedagogical strategy.

Finally, if you still find the observation period frustrating, it may be that you will later realise how useful it was. For example, one trainee we talked to, who had initially been frustrated at being unable to take a more leading role in the classroom during his early school-based experiences, reflected that had he been asked to teach sooner he would not have been ready to do so. He also suggests that the programme of lead-in activities suited his needs, although he became aware of this only with hindsight.

> It was very teacher led . . . he would ask me to concentrate on, say, addition or subtraction, work through it with [small groups] and give them lots of examples and just keep doing it until they're almost fed up . . . At that time I felt quite frustrated, but now I feel that it suited me and possibly because I was going in feeling quite nervous . . . I had to gradually take it in and finally fell on my feet. Looking back now, I think if you'd asked me to teach sooner, I would have found it perhaps much more difficult.
>
> (Male, 30–34, primary)

3 Difficulties making the transition to a teacher role

Some trainees reported difficulties in making the transition to a teaching role. For example, some trainees coming from non-education-related career backgrounds talked about specific features of their teaching placement schools that seemed to compare unfavourably with previous working environments. It was suggested by some, for instance, that their placement schools had a more hierarchical structure and/or a less collegial ethos than they had experienced in their previous working environments. The following quotations from two different trainees illustrate the point:

> I'm used to going into businesses and telling people what they're doing wrong and how they should restructure their business. I went to a meeting on how the school was going to make provision for able students. I raised my hand and a teacher commented on why was I giving an opinion when I'm not even a teacher. They are like that.
>
> (Male, 40–44, secondary)

> Just the way departments are organised, it's very strange . . . it just doesn't feel like a very cohesive unit. It doesn't feel like there's a team producing a product . . . it's like there's a load of individuals there and they could be anywhere and that wasn't what I was expecting.
>
> (Male, 40–44, secondary)

Although not all schools will treat trainees in the same way as in the first quote above, it is perhaps worth thinking about how it will feel, if you are an older trainee with life and work experience, to be 'back at the bottom of the ladder' again and in a new system with a management structure that is likely to be different from those you are used to. In other words, it will be important to try to make sense of the context in its own terms. One way of trying to understand the unique culture of the school in which you find yourself might be to adopt something of an anthropologist's approach, and set some time aside to consider how what you notice people say, do and produce might lead you to a better understanding of the ethos and the organisation of the school.

For those of you entering teacher training programmes straight from A-level courses or undergraduate courses, or with little break in between to pursue alternative careers (i.e. less than two years), our research suggests there are two central areas of transition during your early training. These involve:

1. the transition from A-level to undergraduate study, or from undergraduate to graduate-level study; and
2. the introduction to a professional lifestyle and the responsibilities associated with this.

Trainees who expressed concerns about pursuing a degree programme also recalled concerns about the academic element of their programmes.

> You come in and you go to your first lecture and they start bringing in all those things, and start using terminology and it's like 'oh my God, what are they talking about?' and you write it all down . . . You know like science, some of the information you already know but you've forgotten it because you did it at school. I mean I only did it a few years ago in GCSEs . . . so you are trying to remember it . . . It's all a bit overwhelming at first!
>
> (Female, 20–24, primary)

> You know, when you do your first degree you've got so much time, and my dad was really against my first degree because I had so much spare time and he thought you've got to pay all this money to go and then you're not doing anything, and now he's really shocked by how much I'm doing . . . I'm always like working. [My parents] can't believe it really, even they think it's too much.
>
> (Female, 20–24, primary)

> When we first started you used to think, you know when your alarm clock went off early, 'oh this is so annoying' just because you weren't used to getting up that early.
>
> (Female, 20–24, primary)

The main message from these quotes for younger readers is: 'prepare to work hard'! Most ITT programmes *are* hard work and intensive, but you can console yourself with the thought that not only will it qualify you for your chosen career, but it will also prepare you for the rhythms of working life.

Given that, in undertaking ITT and seeking to 'become a teacher', most trainees need to undergo a role-shift from being a non-teacher to being a teacher,[1] it is perhaps unsurprising that many student teachers are pre-occupied with the notion of teacher identity. Our research suggests that student teachers tend to hold one or other of two positions regarding what the process of becoming a teacher might involve, namely (1) actualising an already identified potential, or (2) undergoing a transformation of self in order to 'change into' a teacher. Where are you on this? Do you feel that you are (or will be) developing an aptitude and skills you already have, or do you feel that you will need to change your *self* in order to become a teacher?

For many student teachers, initial perceptions seem to have included a perceived necessity, at least initially, to undergo a transformation of self in the endeavour to become, or *change into*, a teacher. For example, one interviewee spoke about preparing to go into school in acting terms, as if dressing for the part she was playing (as opposed to *being*). Yet, over time, trainees tend to realise that what they need to do is not so much to 'change into' a teacher but to find the teacher in themselves.

> You try to be the type of person you think they want you to be but as time goes on you realise that actually the score has changed. You don't have to be an automated person. You are your own person, you bring all these things to the job, obviously under the confines of the school . . . You have to keep control of your class . . . that's more like a personal confidence thing rather than how I'm supposed to behave in the school. There's no rulebook to say you have to be like this, bringing in your personality to the teaching role is part of how you teach.
>
> (Female, 30–34, primary)

Those interviewees who saw becoming a teacher as building on existing strengths referred most frequently in this context:

* to the possession of a suitable personality, including having a creative side for which teaching would be an outlet;
* to their knowledge of the subject(s) that they would teach; and
* to having identified relevant 'transferable skills'.

What skills, knowledge, attitudes are *you* bringing that you believe you can build on to become a teacher?

Whatever your position, a certain willingness to change, learn new skills and adapt is necessary. A minority of trainees in our study appeared to be less open to the idea of making personal changes:

> I went in with the view that I am a certain personality, I will teach in a certain way, and if they don't like it, then I won't be a teacher, I'll just do it for a year and leave . . . If my personality and way of doing things didn't fit into the system, I'd go back to IT.
>
> (Male, 40–44, secondary)[2]

4 Difficult relationships with mentors and/or other school teachers

People being people it is (unfortunately) likely that some of you will experience (or are experiencing) some difficulties in your relationships with an important group of people in your ITT, namely teachers in your placement or 'teaching practice' schools. You may have been allocated to one teacher whose job (in addition to his or her own teaching and other responsibilities) is to help you learn from your in-school experiences (and possibly also assess your teaching and/or development). In England this person is called a 'mentor' and he or she is expected to both support your professional development and contribute to assessing your work. (In other parts of the world or systems, such a teacher might be called a 'co-operating teacher', 'school-based tutor', 'co-trainer' or 'supervisor'.)

Many of the student teachers we spoke to were able to form good or very good relationships with these people, but for some there were challenges. For example, one mentor seemed reluctant to let the student teacher take on responsibilities in the classroom, and yet another treated the trainee inappropriately.

> In my first placement the teacher didn't want to let go of her class, she loved them too much and it was like 'no, they're mine'.
>
> (Female, 25–29, secondary)

> I mean I don't mind getting her a cup of tea at break but when I was meant to be observing her, when I was in the middle of working with a group for her, and she'd come over and say 'do you mind going and getting me a cup of tea'. I don't feel then I'm being treated like I should be because that's not what I'm there for. I'm there to learn a job.
>
> (Female, 20–24, primary)

The mentor in the first situation is – reasonably – concerned for her pupils' welfare. However, by denying the trainee opportunities to work with the pupils, she is hindering the trainee's learning. Should you find yourself in such a situation, it is important to start a conversation with your mentor, and start it by showing that you understand the teacher's position. You might try explaining to the mentor that you understand he/she is concerned for the pupils and wants the best for them – as you do. You might, for example, offer to team-teach for a while until the teacher feels confident that your teaching would not be harmful for the pupils. You could gently explain that without opportunities to practise under his or her expert guidance you would have to make your mistakes in a situation where there was no-one (like him/her) around to help you remedy these. Of course, you could also talk to your programme leaders and refer to any programme documentation, but a person-to-person talk is perhaps the best way to try to start to resolve the situation. Try to schedule the talk for a time when neither of you is distracted, and don't ambush the teacher/mentor – tell him or her in advance that you want to discuss how you are working together.

We would suggest a similar approach to the trainee in the second situation: schedule a talk, start by trying to show you understand the teacher's position ('I realise you are very busy and having me here adds to your workload . . .'), and go on to explain what it is you want and hoped for from the placement.

Some of the student teachers we talked to said that, more generally, they found their placement schools to be unwelcoming. One trainee, for example, stated that she, and her fellow trainees, were 'shunned in the staffroom':

> The department I was in was very welcoming but none of the other teachers would talk to us and there were five students there, so we were always sticking together but we were in different subjects in five different departments. In general we were shunned in the staffroom and I was like 'maybe that's what it's like in a secondary school, I don't know'. If I was on my own I would find this quite an isolating experience.
>
> (Female, 25–29, secondary)

If you find yourself in such a situation, again we would suggest you try to think about 'the other side'. How might the teachers in the school above be feeling about a group of new people arriving in their staffroom who – for very understandable reasons – were 'sticking together'? Perhaps you could try to start conversations with individual members of staff, if they don't come to you? You could again begin with something like: 'It must feel like an invasion when all the trainees arrive, and although it's nice for us to have each other, I really want and need to be talking to you too.' (We discuss further ideas for forming and maintaining important relationships with the adults in your teaching situation in Chapter 7 of this book.)

We shortly turn to the last two main sources of 'lows' for the trainees in our study – concerns over pupil behaviour and frustration over the relevance of the theoretical aspects of their programmes, each of which is the subject of a separate chapter (Chapters 5 and 6). There are three main reasons why we have dedicated separate chapters to these two issues and an additional chapter to issues around maintaining good relationships in school. The first is that they are all vital to teaching. The second is that they are issues that the student teachers we spoke to have a lot to say about and that, as teachers of teachers, we are familiar with. The third reason is that they are all predictable (or natural) concerns for beginner teachers. Let us try to explain why we say these concerns are predictable and why we address them in the order that we do.

Previous research and literature on stages of teacher development, which our own research supports, has suggested that learner teachers go through successive cumulative phases (Kagan, 1992; Capel, 2001). The argument goes that, for any teacher new to a class or context, the first concern is with acceptance by the community in the role, and the initial focus is therefore on themselves (their identity and performance as a teacher). However, in order to prepare an appropriate climate for learning, a concern with pupil behaviour is swiftly added. Finally, when these two concerns are manageable, attention can turn to pupil learning, which is potentially the stage at which much of what is taught in ITT (the 'theory' about learning and supporting learning) might become relevant for the beginner teacher. It is also, arguably, the stage to aim to reach by the end of your ITT. None of these concerns ever can (or should) completely go away, but they all become more manageable as we gain in experience and skill. So which chapter are you most looking forward to reading (or have you previously turned to and read one of these)? And does this say anything about your stage of development? When might you be ready to read the others?

5 Relationships with pupils

As perhaps might be expected given the concerns about being a teacher that we discussed in Chapter 3, difficulties with pupil behaviour and with obtaining and maintaining a classroom atmosphere conducive to learning were at the root of many of the emotional lows that the trainees we spoke to experienced. For example:

> To start with, I did have a shock actually going into a classroom. The thing that struck me immediately was the noise level, which I found in some classes quite disturbing. And behaviour, I guess, which is another thing I know people talk about but witnessing it is slightly different to hearing about it . . . People talking out of turn or not listening, getting up out of their seats, moving around, disturbing other people.
>
> (Female, 45 or over, secondary)

As noted above, we devote the whole of the next chapter to this topic, and discuss strategies for facing and coping with a wide range of unpredictable pupil behaviours.

6 Frustration caused by a perceived overemphasis on 'theory'

Can you identify with this sentiment? In discussing their early experiences of ITT, many of the student teachers we spoke to were frustrated about what they saw as too much emphasis by their ITT providers on the 'theory' of becoming a teacher and insufficient emphasis on more practical elements. Many trainees failed to recognise or understand the relevance of the theoretical work addressed to the work they would be doing in school classrooms. We introduced this issue in Chapter 3, where we suggested two ways in which to 'see' the relevance of theory. And since we also devote an entire chapter (Chapter 6) to this question, we'll say no more about it here!

We now go on to discuss some more general strategies which the student teachers in our research adopted as a means of dealing with the range of early difficulties that they experienced.

How the trainees we spoke to coped with difficult early experiences of ITT

The student teachers we spoke to had developed a number of coping mechanisms to help them manage their early in-school problems.

Remember you are a learner – and mistakes are inevitable

Some trainees talked about how seeing themselves as engaged in a learning process, with mistakes being part of this, and teaching skills being something that they would build up over time, helped them cope:

> When I went into the school . . . [the teachers] made it look so easy. Anything that came up they had an answer for straightaway . . . I did feel it might be impossible to pick all this up in 12 months. I remember . . . reminding myself that they've been doing it for so many more years . . . I said to myself not to be silly, you're not going to be fantastic on day one. I broke it down to myself block by block.
>
> (Male, 30–34, primary)

Do you see being a student teacher as being about showing that you can teach or learning how to? As suggested earlier and as other research (Edwards and Ogden, 1998) has shown before, in our research we found that some student teachers seemed to be primarily concerned, in their dealings with other teachers in their placement schools, and especially their mentors, with showing that they were competent teachers already, even when they knew that they were not. This then meant they tried to brush under the carpet some problems that they really ought to have been seeking help to deal with.

Careful planning can help – but remember to plan for the unplanned too

Another strategy used by some trainees involved a reliance (or over-reliance) on lesson plans and worksheets. For example, when reflecting on her early teaching experiences, one BA QTS trainee recalled:

> You know, I had ridiculous plans coming out of my ears and you know, even the teachers were kind of laughing and saying 'I can't believe

you plan this much', but then to me it was essential, because I was so nervous I needed the plan to be there so that I knew exactly what I was doing.

(Female, 20–24, secondary)

One trainee recalled a lesson, early in his training, when he realised it was impossible to plan for all eventualities:

The first day everything went, I won't say wrong, but I didn't act like myself. As it went on and you knew exactly what was happening you could plan for things going wrong, you knew what might go wrong, like I've left all the books out and no-one has taken them . . . but then, a little thing I hadn't thought about [happened. A pupil asked] 'can I open the window?' and [the pupil] was on a table about to open a high window.

(Male, 20–24, secondary)

So, although careful planning is important and can help you feel more confident, it is worth remembering that you can never know exactly how the pupils will react on the day. One way to think this through is first to ask yourself 'what if?' questions (imagining as many potential 'disasters' as you can) for every tiny part of your plan, such as 'what if they don't under-stand?' 'what if they need 10 minutes and not 5?' and so on. Then (second) answer yourself, e.g. 'then I will/would . . .'. This again is something you'll get a lot better at doing over time – partly because you'll be able to imagine more accurately the types of things that can go wrong!

Look after yourself!

Finally, if you are finding things stressful and emotionally draining, what-ever the cause, you probably don't need us to say that looking after yourself is important. There are many books you could read on this topic; for exam-ple, Bubb and Early's (2004) *Managing Teacher Workload: Worklife Balance and Wellbeing* is one of the many on this topic. Or, for a meatier read, try Guy Claxton's classic (1989) text *Being a Teacher: A Positive Approach to Change and Stress*, which may be old and not intended for beginner teach-ers but is full of useful wisdom. It is about 'how to be a successful school-teacher in times of uncertainty, change, increased pressures and conflicting demands' (p. 1). Ring any bells?!

Or, you could simply try making 'self' a 'big rock' in your weekly plan-ning: schedule walks or your favourite physical activity, as well as some pampering 'down time'. Stick to this part of your schedule as assiduously as you do to those times dedicated for planning, for example. And if you need any convincing that you should, Claxton tells us that one of the dis-tressing side-effects of stress that teachers report is 'an increasing punitive-ness towards pupils, colleagues and family' (p. 9) – i.e. we get nastier! So remember, if you aren't good to yourself you can't be good for or to others!

It isn't all doom and gloom – there are early highs too!

We hope after all that that at least you are beginning to feel that most of the difficulties you may face (or be facing) are manageable. If you have been reflecting upon – and perhaps feeling down about – the things that have not been going (or might not go) so well, have you also taken the time to consider what *has* been going well (or what the rewards will be)? It is im-portant to put your negative experiences into context, and it is important to remember that you can't expect everything to go smoothly – you are after all attempting to learn a new and complex skill, and nobody ever said teach-ing was easy. No-one can be (or is) expected to get it right straight away, and even those teachers with many years' experience can't be expected to get it right all the time, as you will discover (if you haven't already). So is your glass half empty or half full? For those of you who have already embarked on an ITT programme, what has gone well in your early experiences of ITT and your school placement? Before you say 'nothing', we must point out that this is highly unlikely – there are always *some* positives to take away from your early experiences of ITT. And perhaps the most positive thing of all is that you have the opportunity to learn from all your experiences – both positive *and* negative, and thus to become a better teacher. If you are struggling to think of some of the things that are going well for you, and which might provide you with some comfort, perhaps some of the things that the student teachers in our research identified as positive early experi-ences for them might jog your memory.

Five main sources of 'highs' were identified by the trainees in our study, when talking about their early experiences of ITT. Do some of these apply to you?

I The joy of 'seeing' learning happen

First, although most student teachers encounter some problems with pupil behaviour, most also enjoy *good relations* with at least some pupils and gain satisfaction from the progress they can see some children making under their care, as suggested by the trainee quoted below:

> [W]hen something clicks . . . and [the pupils] realise that all [the] work and effort they've put in throughout the lesson culminates in some-

thing worthwhile and relevant to them . . . you kind of think 'wow breakthrough', definitely.

(Male, 20–24, secondary)

Have you witnessed and been instrumental in any breakthrough moments? Can you see that some of the pupils you have taught have learned things as a result? (Have you been looking out for this?) If you have yet to start, you might like to plan now to notice and celebrate such moments.

2 Supportive mentoring

Second, 39 of the 85 trainees we spoke to talked, without specific prompting, about how their *relationships with their mentors* had had a positive impact on their early experiences. Some of these talked about specific aspects of their relationships with their mentors, or specific ways in which their mentors had helped them, including boosting their confidence, providing strategies and/or support for classroom management, 'being there/available', and offering guidance for managing time and workload. We illustrate some of these points below in the form of extended quotations from six different student teachers:

> There was one particular lesson which hadn't gone very well and there were reasons for it, and apart from that, I hadn't managed the class terribly well so I learnt a bit from that and [my mentor] was very good. She actually had a word with the class afterwards and said 'your behaviour, your concentration, this time wasn't as good as the last time I saw you' . . . So I think that is probably a big advantage to me.
>
> (Female, 40–44, secondary)

> I'd spent one session and it was almost like I was shouting, my voice just rose and rose and at the end of it I was really hot and flustered and my teacher who'd been watching me, she fed back to me afterwards and she gave me some strategies to use and I used them next time and they worked.
>
> (Female, 25–29, secondary)

> I guess the most useful person during that early time was my mentor because that was the person who I . . . always knew was there in school if I did have a problem or something went wrong . . . You know, he'd given me his home phone number, I had ways of contacting him and he'd said to me, you know 'whenever you need to ring me, ring me', so I felt like I could, he made me feel comfortable with that.
>
> (Male, 20–24, secondary)

People moan about paperwork and stuff but I have a really good mentor . . . [with] a good attitude to it all which she's instilling in me, you know 'don't do more than you need to. Get the basics. Yes, you've got to do it properly but there's a way of doing it properly and not stressing out over it.' She's helping me to manage my role from the beginning.

(Female, 20–24, primary)

[My mentor] made me feel like I was valued. It was 'what would you like to do today?' and I'd say 'I'd like to work with this group' and he'd say 'yes'!

(Female, 20–24, primary)

My mentor, the class teacher, he was brilliant, he was just mad, and everything we did was about having fun. He would ask me 'how could we do this so it's really fun, and how can we do this?' . . . It was just brilliant, I was able to put myself into more and I was probably a bit more relaxed because the class was quite relaxed.

(Female, 20–24, secondary)

Have you benefited from the help of your mentor(s) in any of these or any other ways?

3 Supportive school staff

Third, whereas the above findings from our research may provide little comfort to those of you who have poor relations with or feel unsupported by your mentor, perhaps you have more *positive relations* with and/or have received valuable help and assistance from others? Some trainees in our research who reported dysfunctional relationships with mentors suggested that this was compensated for by the assistance and encouragement they had received from *other teachers (and/or leaders)* in their placement schools, as suggested below:

In my placement my class teacher [and mentor] wasn't so great, but the deputy head and a teacher that I had got quite friendly with from Year 1, she was absolutely fantastic and she went through all the planning with me and, because I really did, in my first week, I really did want to throw in the towel and think I'd had enough because I wasn't getting the support.

(Female, 25–29, primary)

The Head was quite young and quite forward thinking and it was very much 'yeah we love [student teachers], bring them in, they've got good

ideas!' . . . So I was really lucky. I think if I had gone into a school
initially that was hostile, that would have probably put me off.

(Female, 20–24, primary)

4 Supportive fellow trainees

Fourth, some student teachers highlighted the importance of relationships
with, or the presence of, *fellow trainees* in relation to their early school
experiences, as illustrated in the following quotations:

> [It was a good] programme that the school created for us, nine PGCE
> students in the school, two in the maths department which is great,
> having somebody else there in the department is really good . . . really
> good.
>
> (Male, 40–44, secondary)

> [I found] other students particularly helpful . . . Having someone to
> talk to when I'm in the school.
>
> (Male, 20–24, secondary)

5 Supportive family members and friends

Finally, some student teachers in our research took comfort from the fact
that they had received support from their *families, friends or loved ones*,
who were willing to help them through difficult times:

> [M]y husband is extremely supportive and he has been really very help-
> ful and I would say that without his support it would have been dif-
> ficult . . . Because it is a difficult thing to do when you have got a family
> and you have got a home . . . there is so much to do. The children
> must have clothes to wear, you know, they must have food to eat and
> somebody has got to do that.
>
> (Female, 35–39, primary)

If you haven't already started your programme, you might think about
alerting family and friends to the fact that you will be needing their support
too, and perhaps explaining why.

Keep your eye on the long-term goal

Though you might have endured some difficult 'early beginnings' to life as
a student teacher and may have had some doubts about the capacity of your
ITT programme and/or the programme personnel to get you where you

want to be, you might want to consider putting your faith in 'the system', which has been shown to work for the vast majority of student teachers in the past, and trusting that the teachers and tutors you are working with know what they are doing. It might be helpful to bear in mind that, when we asked the student teachers who took part in our survey, at the end of their ITT courses, how confident they were that their ITT programme had prepared them to be an effective teacher, 97 per cent (2,882 of 2,967) said that they were 'very' or 'fairly' confident that their ITT programme had prepared them to be an effective teacher (see Table 4.1).

The majority of the student teachers that we interviewed (65 of the 79) also felt ('very' or 'fairly') well prepared to take up a teaching post on completion of their ITT programme, with only five trainees reporting feeling 'not well prepared'. Many trainees talked about how far they had come (or had developed) during their ITT programmes:

> When I first started the course I couldn't imagine that nine months or whatever it is later I'd suddenly be this teacher that's able to go out and do things but I really do feel very prepared now.
>
> (Female, 20–24, primary)

It just *may* be, however, that a few of you reading this are unable to identify any or many plus points about teaching, reckon that none of our suggestions helps, and find that your time in schools, or on ITT more generally, is making you deeply unhappy. If, in addition, you genuinely feel that you have given it a fair chance and that the things that are making you unhappy are unlikely to change (e.g. even if you were in a different school) then withdrawing from your ITT course, or deferring completion of your ITT, may be the best option for you. We discuss this further in Chapter 8.

Table 4.1 *How confident are you, if at all, that your ITT has prepared you to be an effective teacher?*

	No.	%
Very confident	1,494	50
Fairly confident	1,388	47
Not very confident	66	2
Not at all confident	12	(0)
Don't know	7	(0)
No. of cases	2,967	

Percentages do not sum to 100 owing to rounding. (0) signifies less than 0.5.

Conclusion

Having, in this chapter, looked at some of the reasons for the highs and lows associated with student teachers' early experiences of ITT, and made some brief suggestions for how you might deal with these, we now go on, in Chapter 5, to look in more detail at one of these issues, that of pupil behaviour.

Chapter 5

'It wears you down emotionally'

Dealing with issues of pupil behaviour

Introduction

We have seen in previous chapters that the thought of having to deal with 'bad' pupil behaviour tends to be seen as one of the main drawbacks of teaching as a career and one of the main concerns of those about to embark on an ITT programme. We have also seen that the 'ability to maintain discipline in the classroom' was one of the main skills that the student teachers in our research hoped to learn from their ITT. And we also saw in the last chapter that issues relating to pupil behaviour were at the root of some of the emotional 'lows' suffered, in the early stages of their ITT programmes, by many of the student teachers in our research. In this chapter we show that pupil behaviour remains a problem, for some trainees, further into (and, for some, throughout) their ITT programmes. But we also show that:

- not all student teachers see pupil behaviour as a problem (do you?);
- your ITT course tutors and mentors are there to help you to learn to deal with any problems that you do encounter;
- there are a number of strategies that you can adopt both to help you minimise the likelihood of pupil behaviour becoming a problem in your classroom, and to help you to deal with bad behaviour when it does occur.

As always, before reading on you might like to take some time to reflect on your current feelings about this issue. Perhaps you are in a position to compare your pre-course fears with your actual experience. Is pupil behaviour causing you problems? Are you the only teacher in your school having problems getting those pupils or that class settled and ready to learn? If you have had problems with pupils or classes, what have you done about it? Have any of the strategies you have tried appeared to produce the kind of behaviour you wanted? How long has the effect of your strategy lasted? Which strategies were not successful? Why do you think this is? What other strategies might you try instead? What counts as 'bad behaviour' and is it the same everywhere, for everyone? Does it matter (to you, to pupils, to the school, to society) how you respond to 'bad behaviour'? (It might be useful to come back to these questions again after you have read the whole chapter, or even the whole book, and see if your answers are the same.) On the other hand, you might be reading this chapter as part of a process of making up your mind about whether or not to undertake an ITT programme, and asking yourself, for example:

- Will pupils' behaviour really be as bad as I fear?
- What kinds of systems and support will I get?
- How have other trainees coped?

In this chapter we provide food for thought on the questions we have raised above. But before we discuss the problems with pupil behaviour that some of the student teachers in our research experienced (and you may be experiencing), and ways in which they dealt (and you might deal) with such difficulties, let's start on a positive note!

Not everyone finds all pupil behaviour (or all pupils' behaviour) a problem!

When we asked the student teachers we interviewed, at the end of their ITT courses, which aspects of being a teacher they felt confident about or well prepared to undertake, the second most popular response (after 'subject knowledge') was 'classroom and behaviour management' (mentioned by a quarter of those we spoke to). Similarly, in response to an open-ended survey question, almost a fifth (18 per cent) of respondents said that, going into their first teaching post, they regarded their 'ability to maintain discipline in the classroom' as a strength, which was the fifth most frequently mentioned response.

More generally, many of the student teachers we spoke to said that they felt positive about the relationships that they had formed with pupils they had taught during their school-based experiences. Some of them even talked about 'enjoying' pupils' company!

> I did enjoy it actually . . . I mean the kids although they had their problems and there were some really problem children there, it was actually enjoyable. The children in the class were really nice and very sociable and friendly, you know.
>
> (Female, 35–39, secondary)

> I thought I was going to get a class of horrible kids when actually you get a class of kids and they make you smile because some of them are so witty and amusing and funny and nice, and one or two of them are challenging. So that changed the whole idea that all of them would be horrible.
>
> (Female, 45 or over, secondary)

So, the good news is that, for many of the student teachers in our study, the behaviour of the majority of the pupils in their classes was in fact acceptable. But would *you* have thought the same in the same classes? It rather depends, we think, on your expectations and on your thinking. In other words, the extent to which pupil behaviour is acceptable or not has something to do with the way teachers think, as well as what the pupils actually do and say. Let's explain a bit more what we mean: if you think back to your own school days, we are sure you remember classes where the teacher let you 'get away with' more than ('stricter') teachers in other classes. In other words, the same behaviour was seen as 'a problem' by one teacher and not by another – though in some cases it may have been the case that the behaviour was *noticed* by one teacher and not by another, or was noticed by both teachers but one teacher was 'better' than the other at managing it! We also expect that for some of those classes where you (or others) could 'get away' with more than in the classes of the 'stricter' teachers, in the long term it got in the way of your learning, whereas for other such classes it didn't affect your learning. And we expect that, in the classes of 'strict' teachers, some of the behaviour that was frowned upon (perhaps a quick whisper to a neighbour) would have helped your learning (if it was to check your understanding of a task you had just been set, for example), whereas in other such classes the calm ordered atmosphere was helpful to you. So, a good idea might be to decide (and visualise or imagine, perhaps using examples from your observation period), what kind of behaviour you would ideally want, and why.

For us, the main criterion for deciding whether a particular piece of behaviour is acceptable or not relates to whether or not it supports learning – the individual's or that of others. That was easy to write but it is not always as easy to determine in practice. As we suggested earlier, the profession is constantly finding different explanations for how learning (and the differentiated support for learning that different subjects require) occurs. And young people are not only learning their subjects. School is a place for 'secondary socialisation' (the primary source being the home and home community). In other words, they are also 'learning adulthood' – and this is particularly evident in the teenage years, when the phase of development is one of moving towards independence from adult 'carers' (teachers, parents).

In dealing with teenagers, we have found it helpful to remember that, as with any learning process, 'mistakes' in learning adulthood – or inappropriate choices of behaviour – are inevitable. In fact, when some pupils display the kind of behaviour that you, their classmates, or the school deem to hinder learning, there may be one or more of a whole variety of potential explanations for such behaviour. Potential explanations might, for example, relate to their personal characteristics (from personality type to difficulties categorised under 'Special Educational Needs'), or in some cases it may be that they have simply not yet had the opportunities in their lives to learn appropriate behaviour for learning in schools.

We shortly discuss concrete ways student teachers in our study coped with – and strategies for dealing with – inappropriate pupil behaviour, but here it is worth noting that, as a starting point, it will be important to try to understand and build a relationship with all pupils. Again, as many as 36 per cent of respondents to our survey said that, going into their first teaching posts, their 'Ability to develop productive relationships with pupils' was a strength, and this was the joint highest response (along with their subject knowledge). Some of the student teachers in our research acknowledged that teacher educators associated with their ITT programme should take some of the credit for this. As one of these trainees put it:

> I've had plenty of support in terms of behaviour management from the school and both my mentor and the heads of year and the pastoral system. Behaviour management I feel very happy about.
>
> (Male, 40–44, secondary)

So, perhaps it isn't all as difficult as you might have been thinking. As we have seen, not all student teachers see pupil behaviour as a problem, and part of the job of the teachers and tutors associated with your ITT course is to help you develop appropriate skills for dealing with this and other aspects of the work of being a teacher. We said above that different teachers might view the same pupil behaviour differently – so too might different schools (or school policies). In addition, the potential for unacceptable pupil behaviour (perhaps because of the typical home backgrounds of pupils in the school) can also vary a great deal from one school to the next. So, if you are having problems with this issue just now, you might not do so if/when you move to another school (and vice versa!). But remember, even if the potential for unacceptable pupil behaviour is just as bad (or worse) at your next school, you will be more experienced and better equipped to understand it (and the pupils who display such behaviour), and so to minimise its occurrence and to take appropriate courses of action to deal with it when it does occur. In other words, not only will how you as a teacher think about the behaviour of pupils develop as you revisit the questions 'is it acceptable?', 'does it support learning?', etc. but, with experience, so too will your repertoire of strategies.

... but some pupil behaviour *is* inappropriate!

If you are a student teacher in school, do you sometimes feel you must have a large placard with 'student teacher – behave badly here' on your back? In spite of the 'good news' we talked about in the last section, unfortunately many student teachers do endure some miserable experiences due to the behaviour of some of the pupils they are trying to teach. One student teacher we spoke to referred to his first placement as 'a horrific experience', largely on account of having to face 'unruly' pupils. Another trainee said:

> [The placement I'm in] it's just got incredibly poor discipline and behaviour problems . . . People kind of think 'oh you know, they're only students what can they do?' But if it's different students all the time giving you lip . . . it wears you down emotionally . . . There are days when I just come home thinking 'bloomin heck', you know, almost in tears, going 'I can't do this'.
>
> (Male, 20–24, secondary)

Furthermore, although most student teachers, assisted by their ITT mentors and tutors, were able to improve their behaviour management skills during the course of their ITT programmes, 'the ability to maintain discipline in the classroom' was identified as the third biggest area in which our survey respondents felt they would benefit from additional training or development (after the 'ability to work with pupils with special educational needs (SEN) and inclusion'), going into their first year of teaching. (Incidentally, 22 per cent of those seeking posts in secondary schools reported that they would benefit from additional training or professional development in the 'ability to maintain discipline in the classroom', compared with a relatively low 12 per cent of those seeking posts in primary schools. This supports the view that the behaviour of teenagers tends to be seen as more of a problem than that of younger children, largely because the particular developmental phase they are in, on the 'learning adulthood' journey, is one of striving for independence and 'trying on' different adult identities.)

We should point out, too, that some of the trainees we spoke to were critical of their ITT courses for not giving sufficient coverage to this (behaviour management) issue, or for not supporting their learning in sufficiently meaningful ways for them:

> I don't think they do very much on behaviour, classroom behaviour management. They do spend a bit of time on it but really it is a big, big issue, without that you can't do anything else really. Nothing is going to work without that, so I think probably there could have been a lot more on that.
>
> (Male, 35–39, secondary)

> [T]here are various points along the way where I thought I could really do with some more . . . ideas about, you know, classroom management strategies and dealing with kids who don't respond to the normal kind of four-point discipline – first warning, second warning, stand

up, stand out, and all that kind of stuff. But that was because I was in schools where there were a lot of kids who just didn't respond to those kind of warnings.

(Female, 20–24, secondary)

If you feel the same about your own course: first, don't be afraid to ask your tutors and mentors; and, second, read on! In the next section we outline some of the strategies that the student teachers we spoke to found useful in helping them to deal with problematic behaviour, and we offer some additional suggestions for understanding and managing pupil behaviour, based on our own and other writers' experience.

What helped the trainees in our research?

The student teachers we talked to identified six main strategies (not all of which we would unequivocally support!) that they felt helped them to improve their behaviour management skills or to 'deal with' poor pupil behaviour. We discuss each of these in turn.

I Observe the experts

The biggest single thing that seemed to help the trainees we talked to to improve their behaviour management skills was observing experienced and expert classroom practitioners at work. When we asked one trainee whether she could identify any significant moments or activities during the year which influenced her development as a teacher, she discussed how, after 'struggling a little bit to keep the class under control' in her first placement, she went to observe 'an excellent teacher, who had excellent classroom management skills', and subsequently benefited from her later attempts to adopt some of the approaches that she had seen:

> In the end I actually didn't teach for half the lesson, to a couple of groups that seemed quite difficult and just spent pretty much half an hour or so on what I expected in the classroom and behaviour and from that point, it did turn, it was better . . . I think it was basically getting them to come in the classroom quietly and sit down and then you could lay out what the lesson was going to be about and also get them to be quiet at the end of the lesson before they left. It did seem to make a big difference.
>
> (Female, 45 or over, secondary)

Another student teacher said:

I have been very lucky with the teacher I've been placed with. Her behaviour management is superb. The course did give us [lectures] on behavioural management but obviously it was very general but my teacher uses a lot of non-verbal techniques to start them working and to quieten them down [and] I've never shouted since I've been there . . . It's very nice and calming. It's really nice to see that in action.

(Female, 20–24, primary)

How do you (or can you imagine) beginning and ending lessons? What kind of non-verbal techniques could you try using to signal your expectations or instructions to the pupils? What effects might these have? Are there any teachers whose behaviour management techniques you have not observed but would like to observe? (Can your mentor or tutor recommend any?) Have you asked any of those teachers yet?

2 Don't be too friendly

Some student teachers spoke about how they had benefited from adopting a slightly more 'authoritative' approach after initially suffering from trying to become the pupils' friend or not being sufficiently 'strict':

I was used to speaking to the children in a certain way, being more like a friend than a teacher. [When I started in school] I had children coming up and hugging me and talking about what they did at the weekend and then when I had to teach them at the end of the second week there were discipline problems because I hadn't got the right respect and showed them what my role was . . . I knew I'd done wrong and I changed and I took on an authoritative role and that worked and now my role is completely as a teacher.

(Female, 20–24, primary)

I think, bizarrely, a happy class is one that you are in control of and you are quite strict with . . . I think certainly I know from my last practice, when things were going mad in my class there were a lot of children who looked unhappy and they were putting up their hands saying I want to learn, I want to learn, and that was because of the conditions in that class.

(Male, 25–29, primary)

Other trainees who had adopted a 'sterner' approach from the outset talked about how, once they had established themselves with the pupils, and established that they were 'in charge', they were then able to become slightly less authoritarian:

I have been able to sort of relax more with the pupils and actually develop a bit of a rapport and a bit of a relationship with them, and perhaps not be as sort of distant as I was to start off with.

(Female, 25–29, secondary)

Some of these trainees may have been adhering to the popular tip: 'don't smile before Christmas' (i.e. the end of the first term). Yet another beginner teacher, who had worked as a social worker with disturbed youth before training to teach, told us later in our research (when he had been teaching for two years) that this was 'the most ridiculous piece of advice in the world', and advice that his ITT course leader had advised him and his fellow trainees *not* to listen to.

Beginning teachers will often see-saw between authoritarian, all-powerful 'do as I say, or else' approaches, and '*laissez-faire*' approaches such as 'I want you to like me so I'll let you do as you like'. The first may create the conditions for subject learning but, in the long term, impedes not only the 'learning adulthood' project but even, for some pupils' at least, their motivation for learning the subject. The second may allow some learning adulthood realisations, for those old enough to have them, but will almost certainly impede subject learning, in the short term at least. The approach we all need to strive for, we think, is an authoritative (not authoritarian) one – one in which you command respect. How you earn that respect (for it will need to be earned) will be different for each of you and may differ from school to school, class to class or pupil to pupil, but it will certainly involve both demonstrating your knowledge of, and enthusiasm for, the subject(s) you are teaching and demonstrating your respect for and interest in your pupils and their learning – including by ensuring that there are appropriate conditions for that learning in the class. So, in order to show respect for pupils' learning, and if, unlike the beginner teacher quoted above, you have had little prior experience of working with groups of young people, the ideas *behind* the old advice about not smiling until the end of the first term *may* be appropriate for you (see 'Start right' in the More Tips section below).

3 *Plan interesting lessons to motivate your pupils and be enthusiastic*

As we said above, one way to earn the respect of the pupils is by demonstrating that you care about/are genuinely interested in both them and their learning and the subject you teach. As two of our research participants put it:

It has to be fun, the children have to enjoy it. Making it as enjoyable as you can, they'll be more interested, more motivated. You've got to motivate them so that they will learn.

(Female, 45 or over, primary)

I always thought you're going to have to be interesting . . . you're going to have to engage the kids.

(Male, 40–44, secondary)

4 Model appropriate behaviour – mutual respect

Student teachers in our study also talked about the need for mutual respect between pupils and between teacher and pupils, with behaviour that demonstrated a lack of respect being therefore unacceptable.

I think making them feel safe as well, creating like a safe, positive environment and reinforcing positive behaviour and not allowing children to be negative about each other in that environment because that happens quite easily as well, just sort of laughing at each other. Obviously if it's funny and you're all laughing together it's different.

(Female, 25–29, secondary)

Rather than a friend they should have respect for you, but you should get on with each other really. I think mutual respect. I have got to respect others, pupils, and they have got to have respect for me.

(Female, 20–24, secondary)

5 Hide the student teacher badge!

Some of the student teachers we talked to felt that (as we briefly suggested above) potential problems with pupil behaviour might be exacerbated by pupils' knowledge that you are a student teacher. They thus sought not to draw attention to this fact and to act and behave, in front of the pupils, like a 'real' teacher. This is illustrated in the following quotation (if you thought that 'hide the badge' in the sub-title above was a metaphor, you will see that this trainee really had been given a 'student teacher' badge to wear!):

I think if the children know, especially the older children, if they find out that you're a student . . . they tend to try and wind you up basically. We were given a badge . . . and it said 'graduate teacher training programme' and I just thought 'I am not wearing it' so it got shoved in the bag and left there until I left because I just thought that is going to be a hurdle for me to get over.

(Female, 25–29, primary)

Although we wouldn't want *you* (or your mentors/tutors) to forget that you are a student teacher and a *learner*, we tend to agree that not drawing attention to 'the student teacher badge', if you can get away with it, is a useful one – and at least one of us used this strategy *himself* as a student teacher!

6 Blame it on the pupils!

One strategy adopted by some trainees who were experiencing problems with pupil behaviour was to identify this as characteristic to their placement school or to a particular group of pupils, rather than being related to their own teaching skills. For example, one trainee recalled:

> I did a lesson with my boss observing. It didn't go brilliantly, it felt like the opening scene from *Saving Private Ryan* and she took the next half of the lesson. It was Year 9, very difficult kids, but I coped!
>
> (Male, 40–44, secondary)

In some ways, this strategy might have helped some trainees to cope with the difficulties they were facing. It might, for example, have been reassuring to them or less damaging to their confidence at this stage to place the responsibility in the hands of the pupils they were attempting to teach (while learning how to teach). And in some cases and in some respects it *is* sometimes a 'pupil' issue, illustrated by the fact that even more experienced teachers can have problems with 'those' pupils (this can be reassuring!).

On the other hand, thinking in this way and not taking at least some responsibility for the less appropriate behaviour occurring in your classes might present an obstacle to your learning and development. As a general rule we'd say, if you find yourself talking or thinking about 'difficult kids' – rather than 'difficult behaviour' or 'children who display a lot of unacceptable behaviour' – you are engaged in what is known as 'labelling', and this can have negative effects. It can, for example, even create the opposite effects from those you want: all people to a greater or lesser extent (but younger ones in particular) strive to live up to expectations, and so, if you expect them to be difficult, they might be more likely to actually be difficult! If, on the other hand, you see their behaviour, rather than them, as 'difficult' (for whom?), or as being an inappropriate choice (a mistake in the learning adulthood journey), you may be able to think of a way to offer them an alternative and more appropriate way of behaving.

Having talked about some of the strategies for dealing with pupil behaviour mentioned by some of the student teachers in our research, we now introduce some additional suggestions which you might find helpful.

More tips

Many of the recommendations in this section expand on and develop the ideas already mentioned above. They are drawn not only from our own experience, but also from many useful books and articles we have read on the topic, and because of this we have included a selected annotated bibliography at the end of this chapter.

Start right

This is as important to remember for the initial phases of work with a class as for the start of every lesson. We expect you know the importance of first impressions, so how you present and introduce yourself to your pupils matters, even down to how you dress. Bennett (2008) suggests, 'close your eyes and imagine what a teacher with great control looks like. Then go to the wardrobe and dress like it.' Many other authors also suggest 'hide the badge' tactics, recommending, for example, that no matter how nervous (or angry, or hurt) you may feel it will be important to act as if you weren't – at least at the start. Later, when you have established productive relationships with the class and the individuals in it, it may be appropriate to say something like 'I feel X, when you do Y', but often they will need to be convinced first that you care about how *they* feel before they will care about how *you* feel as a result of their behaviour – and that can take time. In this context, many advise that beginner teachers should 'try to avoid saying "I'll get Miss/Sir if you don't behave"' (Bennett, 2008), as this suggests that you are not 'in charge' – someone else is! This is not to say that you should not get all the help you can or need, just that in this in-class scenario it is best to 'use others as a last resort' (Bennett, 2008).

Part of 'starting right' will be to ensure that everyone in the class knows and understands how they are expected to behave and what any consequences for not doing so will be. It may not be enough to simply refer the class to the school behaviour policy, not only because different teachers will inevitably notice different things and be more or less tolerant but also because slightly different norms may be appropriate for the learning of different subjects (for example, it's hard to imagine effective learning going on in a silent modern foreign language class, and agreements may need to be made on whether, when and for how long the use of English, or the mother tongue, is acceptable). You may choose to simply state what you expect but, perhaps especially with older classes, compliance may be more forthcoming (and the influential power of group pressure brought to bear) if class rules are *negotiated*.

One way of developing negotiated class rules might be via a 'pyramid discussion', preferably in the first lesson with a new class, which begins with you asking the pupils to think about the conditions they need for their learning of your subject in class and to note down individually, say, five 'rules' they would like to have respected by all. Pupils are then grouped and asked to share what they have written and come to an agreement on a maximum of, say, three rules that they all think are important for their learning. Groups then report the outcomes and a list is drawn up of the collected suggested class rules. You can veto any that contradict the school policy, explaining why, and add one or two perhaps if need be. The next stage is to obtain agreement from everyone that they will endeavour to stick to these rules, which the class has decided they need if they are to learn well. Finally, you might also seek to have the class work out together (in plenary or in a similar pyramid discussion process) what the consequences for not adhering to the rules will be and when and how warnings are given, though again you may need to feed in to this process to ensure that relevant school policies are not contradicted. The outcomes of this process might then be posted somewhere prominent and referred to by you (and often a transgressor's classmates) as and when appropriate.

As we suggested above, the start of *every lesson* is also very important. Bennett (2008) also suggests that you should:

- 'Be in the classroom before your pupils, preferably at the door'.
- 'Have every resource you need on your desk before they get there'.
- 'If anyone is messing around as they enter, ask them to wait outside, calmly and always politely. They need to learn from the start that you have high expectations.'

All of the above indicates that you will have a fair bit of planning and preparation to do before any 'start' if you are to do it 'right'. But with experience and reflection, you *will* manage these starts more effectively.

Be consistent

Our experience (and every other book we have read) tells us that it is really important that you are consistent. If you are inconsistent it sends a message that you didn't really mean it and more and more pupils will break rules and the whole system breaks down. The only option then is to start again. Being consistent is quite a challenge for all of us when we begin teaching, in part because it may initially require us to engage in what feels unlike normal human interactions. For example, if the class has been told or agreed that pupils must raise their hand if they want to speak, and wait to be nominated before doing so, then should anyone speak or shout out without doing so, at the very least you need to ignore them completely, and consistently ignore them until they realise you meant it.

Being consistent also means (as we suggested above) adhering to the school behaviour policy. (In England currently, most of these adopt a 'limit-setting' approach[1]). Pupils learn acceptable behaviour in every class, and will do so more easily if every teacher 'sings from the same hymn sheet'. So if, by any chance, you disagree with any aspect of the policy, or with the approach and thinking underlying it, seek to discuss it and change it. If you simply flout it in your class you will probably be doing your colleagues and your pupils a disservice.

Model the behaviour you expect (and practise what you preach)

Bennett (2008) suggests that pupils 'deserve the kind of manners that you expect from them'. Not only do they deserve them, but they *need* them both to feel your respect for them and – and this is really important – to learn appropriate adult behaviour. Pupils will learn a lot from how you behave as well as from what you tell them.

So it is with every piece of expected behaviour or class rule. If, for example, you expect pupils to listen to you, you will need to listen to them. And you need to listen to them not only to model the kind of respectful behaviour you want, but also because you need to understand them, to understand how they are feeling and thinking, in order to work out how to support their learning.

Don't raise your voice (or don't raise it too often!)

In a sense, advice to refrain from shouting or raising your voice could be seen as being part of the tips provided above: even if you are angry, don't show it, and if you don't want the pupils to shout, you shouldn't shout. But there are other very good reasons why it is inadvisable to shout or raise your voice. We are reminded of the old saying 'a noisy teacher makes a noisy class', and if you simply want, for example, to stop group work and take the floor and shout to make yourself heard over the hubbub, you might like to think of non-verbal strategies for gaining attention in such circumstances. You could, for example, agree that the signal to finish the sentence, stop talking and pay attention to the teacher will be a bell, or a piece of music, or your raised hand.

Other reasons for not raising your voice are that, if you do so, you may induce fear (particularly perhaps if you are male), and this will impede learning and/or sound as if you have lost control, which won't help class management. Not raising your voice may also help you avoid the voice problems (loss of voice) that many beginner teachers in our research study experienced, as when people often shout or raise their voices, this can not only sound rather unpleasant, but also strain and severely damage their vocal cords.[2] Finally, when we raise our voices our voice changes – we are not in our normal tone and our resonance is affected – so our voice may be less, not more, effective.

Having said all that, some experienced teachers prefer to 'never say never' and to reserve the right to raise their voices – or even 'shout' – on rare occasions (e.g. as a last, or almost last, resort), when they feel the situation merits this! However, such a strategy will be more effective where it is *controlled projection* rather than an involuntary expression of anger.

Keep striving to understand your pupils and the reasons behind their behaviour

When asked, pupils always include 'fair' in their list of adjectives describing 'good' teachers. Part of being 'fair' is being consistent. If you say, or it is agreed, that certain behaviour is expected and other types of behaviour are not tolerated, then the agreed or appropriate consequences for rule-breaking should always follow. The strict teacher who didn't allow the whisper that might have helped learning (as described above) was certainly being consistent, but was she or he being 'fair'? It might have been helpful to the teacher to know why the pupil felt the need to whisper. If, for example, it was because he/she had misunderstood instructions or was unclear about what to do next (in which case other pupils might be in the same boat), then knowing this would prompt you to restate the instructions, or ask another pupil to do so, which would serve to facilitate learning.

It is important to recognise, too, that pupils may not themselves be clear about why they behave as they do, and here is where your learning about your pupils' backgrounds, and your reading about the age group you are teaching (their stage of development and associated learning adulthood 'tasks') or identifiable indicators suggesting named syndromes in the 'Special Educational Needs' spectrum will be helpful. It is important to think about understanding *all* your pupils and *all* their behaviour. Although the 'naughty' children will undoubtedly take a lot of your spare thinking time, don't ignore the quiet compliant child hidden in the middle of the class – is her behaviour always supportive of her own or her classmates' learning too?

One tool for thinking and understanding human behaviour that we have found really useful is described by Glasser (1998). He sees all behaviour as fundamentally striving to meet basic psychological needs (BPNs). Adults and carers take charge of helping us meet those needs up to the point when, as teenagers, we start trying to meet them for ourselves – but of course, as with any learning, from time to time we will make mistakes or inappropriate choices of ways to do so. For Glasser, there are five BPNs. The first is a need for *security*. Fortunately, in most parts of the world and in most schools physical security is not a big issue; rather, as one of the trainees we quoted above realised, it is a case of trying to ensure that the classroom is a psychologically safe place, where everyone is respected, there are no 'put-downs' from either classmates or teacher, and no-one is laughed at (particularly important when less than perfection and mistakes are inevitable). The second BPN is a need for *belonging*, the third is for *success* or achievement, the fourth is for *freedoms* or choices, and the fifth for *fun*.

Could some of the unacceptable behaviours displayed by the young people in your class be explained as inappropriate choices for meeting one or more of these BPNs? If so, could you help them meet them more appropriately by changing what you do or say or how you plan? Are you helping your pupils notice and celebrate genuine achievements as well as where there is 'room for improvement'? Do you remember to 'catch them doing something right'? Do you give your teenage class choices and options? Do you have a range of 'learning through fun' strategies you can draw on in your planning or spontaneously if meeting that need seems to be a priority? (Teenage years are pressured in the run-up to important exams, and these young people are not yet adults – even though many may strive to think of themselves as such – and are not long past the phase when play was the principal means of learning.) Do you pay attention to group dynamics and to ensuring that all can meet their need for belonging in your class? One of us consistently used (and uses) this (BPN) 'tool for thinking' when checking plans and makes adjustments to try to ensure that there are opportunities for all these needs to be met by every pupil in every lesson, or at least in every unit.

Conclusion

In this chapter we have addressed one of the major sources of anxiety and emotional 'lows' encountered by student teachers, namely issues relating to pupil behaviour. We have tried to emphasise that not all pupils behave inappropriately, that part of the job of your ITT tutors and mentors is to help you develop appropriate skills of behaviour management, and that many student teachers complete their ITT programmes feeling that they have indeed developed the ability to manage pupil behaviour – to such an extent that they regard it as one of their strengths. We have also acknowledged, however, that some pupils do behave inappropriately (at least some of the time), and we have offered both a number of ways of thinking about pupil behaviour and a number of practical strategies that we hope you will find helpful should you encounter what you consider to be inappropriate behaviour in your classrooms. For those of you who remain concerned and/or wish to learn more about this issue, we provide a brief introduction to some additional sources of potential help under 'Further reading' below. But for those who wish to go straight there, in the next chapter we return to – and address in detail – another common source of frustration felt by student teachers, that relating to the relevance and value of 'theory' in ITT.

Further reading

Dillon, J. and Maguire, M. (Eds) (2007) *Becoming a Teacher: Issues in Secondary Teaching*. Maidenhead: Open University Press.

This edited collection draws on a wide body of educational research as well as the professional experience of the different contributors. Burke's chapter, 'Classroom management', emphasises the need for teachers to think in terms of promoting learning rather than controlling behaviour, and contains practical illustrations. As the title suggests, this book is more appropriate for those of you becoming (or considering becoming) secondary teachers.

Gootman, M. E. (2001) *The Caring Teacher's Guide to Discipline: Helping Young Students Learn Self-control, Responsibility, and Respect*. Thousand Oaks, CA: Corwin.

As the foreword says, 'this book is thoughtful, practical, and extremely respectful of teachers and of the multiple judgements needed to educate young children well'. The author starts with the stated premise that 'children are not born bad'. (Do you agree? If you do, do you nonetheless sometimes *expect* some children to be 'naughty'? Remember the power of expectations!) The book includes chapters containing useful practical tips and strategies for dealing with low-level disruptions or 'chronic misbehaviours' of younger pupils, such as 'tattling' or bullying. One to dip in and out of.

Humphreys, T. (1998) *A Different Kind of Discipline*. Dublin: Newleaf.

Written by a psychologist, this book addresses what is referred to as 'undercontrolled' and 'overcontrolled' behaviour. (Perhaps that quiet, compliant child 'hidden' in the middle of the class in fact displays over-controlled behaviour?) The author usefully identifies examples of teacher behaviours that can, through being over- or undercontrolled, lead to problems with pupil behaviour. The author also discusses possible origins in the child and the home environment of behaviour issues, and proposes useful practical strategies for all concerned.

Porter, L. (2000) *Behaviour in Schools: Theory and Practice for Teachers*. Buckingham: Open University Press.

This book discusses different approaches to both understanding and dealing with issues relating to pupil behaviour and provides evidence on the short-term and long-term impact of these. It can challenge your thinking as well as give you some useful strategies that are associated with different approaches to dealing with issues of pupil behaviour. It's quite meaty, so not really a 'dip in and out' kind of book, but one we would recommend you look at while you have time, perhaps in preparation for an assignment on your ITT course.

Chapter 6

'All the theory goes out of the window'?

The relevance and value of theory in ITT

Introduction

In Chapter 3 we showed that, before they begin ITT courses, most people expect to learn most from the more practical aspects of their programmes, those more directly concerned with in-class teaching, and many are sceptical about the more theoretical elements of course provision. We also suggested two useful ways of thinking about theory or of seeing those parts of your course which are less obviously and directly connected with in-class teaching, which might help you to understand their relevance and might be helpful to your learning and your teaching. By way of a brief reminder, we suggested that 'theories' could be seen:

- as possible 'explanations' of events that occur in (your or others') classrooms; and
- as 'tools' which might be used in planning teaching.

In Chapter 4 too we discussed how some trainees we talked to spoke about their dissatisfaction with theoretical aspects of the early stages of their ITT programmes, notably where they could not see the relevance of this to their work in school classrooms.

In this chapter we discuss this important (relevance of theory) question in more detail. In particular, we would like to:

- share with you how the student teachers in our research felt about this issue by the end of their ITT programmes; and
- suggest ways in which those of you who have made the decision to undertake ITT or who are currently following an ITT programme can learn from their experiences and make the most of course theory.

So, for those of you who are part-way though your ITT course:

- What do you presently understand by theory and what purpose do you think it serves?

- Do you think it is (or has been) useful to think about theory as possible 'explanations' of classroom events as you reflect on these, or as tools for planning teaching, as we suggested?
- How, if at all, have particular theories influenced how you plan, teach or assess your pupils' work?
- Do you still find 'theory' generally impractical, and perhaps even suspect that we (the authors of this book) are out of touch with the realities of teaching?!

If you (still) can't understand the relevance of theory, this is not particularly unusual . . . and there is still time!

What is theory?

If 'theory' is one part of what your course provides, how would you refer to the rest? Many of the student teachers in our research saw the content of their ITT course in terms of 'theory' and 'practice', with the latter referring to 'practical' aspects such as classroom teaching or activities that enabled them to observe, discuss or simulate concrete instances of teaching and learning. In general, trainees used the term 'theory' to refer to a broad range of knowledge including, for example:

- 'content' knowledge about the subjects they were training to teach;
- knowledge about lesson planning, assessment and how to differentiate work;
- knowledge of the National Curriculum;
- knowledge about how children learn, including research findings and the study of aspects of child psychology.

Yet not everyone we spoke to saw 'theory' in the same way, as we explain below.

Contrasting views on the relevance of theory

I Theory as irrelevant

Many (though not all) student teachers in our research were sceptical of the value of some 'theoretical' elements of ITT programmes because they did not recognise their relevance to or implications for their work as teachers. In our survey of student teachers at the end of their ITT courses, only 18 per cent of respondents said that the links between the theoretical and practical elements of their ITT programmes were 'always clear', with 67 per cent stating that the links were 'usually' clear, 14 per cent saying that they were 'often not clear', and 1 per cent (22 of the 3,154 respondents who answered this question) stating that the connections between theory and practice were 'never clear'! One of the trainees we spoke to saw much of what she was learning as relevant only in obtaining the certificate (which 'qualifies' her to teach) and for use in job interviews. Another trainee, when talking about theories such as constructivism (have you come across this theory yet?), said that 'real teachers' in 'real schools' 'don't relate to that any more' as they are 'in there doing a real job'. The views of two other student teachers are illustrated in the quotations given below:

> When all is said and done you are actually training to teach so all the theory goes out the window when you're actually stood in front of a class full of children.
>
> (Female, 30–34, secondary)

> For the life of me, I don't see the relevance of assignments to the real world. I mean, I don't see it because it is just, I have gone to read something and I am just regurgitating it onto a piece of paper.
>
> (Female, 30–34, primary)

Those elements of course provision which trainees tended to regard as more 'relevant' included work undertaken in relation to classroom management and trainees' subject specialisms:

> I think the most useful [part of the course] is actually doing the teaching practices and the [university] instruction in the lesson preparation and classroom behaviour and behaviour management.
>
> (Female, 45 or over, secondary)

Do any of the words from the trainees we spoke to and quoted above ring any bells? Are any of them similar to thoughts you have had? Or do you identify more closely with the views of those trainees we quote below?

2 Theory as relevant

Not all the student teachers in our research failed to see the relevance or the benefits of the theory that they encountered on their ITT course. Among those trainees who saw theory as useful and relevant to their (classroom) practice, some had *entered* ITT with the belief that theory would help them to understand and develop their in-school experiences, whereas others (and most) had come to see connections between theory and practice *after* they had begun their ITT programmes, especially after gaining some practical experience in schools. These student teachers talked about:

- being able to put their HEI-based learning 'into practice'; and
- being able to 'see theory in practice' or see empirical support in their placement schools for particular theories about teaching and learning.

Two quotations from trainees who were initially doubtful but subsequently came to see the relevance and value of theory are given below:

> I think one of the things that really hit home is that you learn quite a lot while you're at university but it never really, like you can say you understand it, but it never really makes sense until you're in a school situation, I don't think, and I think that you can forget things, go into school and do something and your mentor says 'you could do this' and you think 'I learnt that at university but I'd just forgotten it' because it has no real relevance till you're in school I don't think.
>
> (Female, 20–24, secondary)

> The theory side of things, like the constructivist theory is something that I've really taken on board and it's something that at the time when they told me as a theory I didn't understand it and I thought 'why am I learning this? This doesn't apply to me.' But actually as I've developed as a teacher . . . I've thought 'oh hang on, the thing I believe in relates to this theory' so . . . on reflection it was good that we had that because now I can see where to take it from the theory, or [how] to extend it in different ways.
>
> (Female, 20–24, primary)

Those of you who may be thinking that there is 'too much theory' on your programme might be interested to learn that some of the trainees in our research who were following employment-based ITT programmes actually wanted *more* theory, and some really valued the encounters with 'theory' that they had. Hence, almost a third (31 per cent) of those trainees following Graduate or Registered Teacher Programmes in England felt (unlike those following all other ITT routes) that the balance between the theoretical and practical aspects of their programme was too heavily weighted towards the practical. One GTP trainee whom we spoke to was particularly appreciative of the taught sessions (in which 'theory' is most likely to be encountered), and valued being able to stand back from and theorise practice.

> The taught sessions have been useful, the input we've had in college. I mean there are so many things that you feel you need to have in place before you actually get in [to the classroom] but in some ways you realise that you appreciate [these things] better when you come in to discuss them in the uni.
>
> (Female, 40–44, primary)

Where do you stand now?

So where do *you* stand on the relevance of theory debate? Do you sympathise more with the views of the first group of student teachers quoted above or the second? If you too are a theory-sceptic at this point in time, this is entirely understandable. Yet we think there are ways of understanding the words of the theory-sceptics we quoted above which both make the speakers 'right' *and* challenge whether this necessarily means that 'theory' is in fact irrelevant! For example, we think it's quite normal that theory often 'goes out of the window' when in the midst of teaching: there often isn't the time or opportunity to stop and think in the kind of logical way that taking a considered account of theory would need. It is *before* lessons, in the planning, and *after* lessons, when working out why things happened as they did, that we can make conscious use of what we know theoretically. And by drawing on theory in this way in our planning and in our reflection on practice, it can then have a beneficial (practical) effect on our subsequent teaching efforts – even though, again, we may not always consciously consider theory *during* the lessons.

We also agree that 'regurgitating' what you read for assignments (as one of the trainees we quoted above put it) is not necessarily a very useful activity, though it is highly unlikely that this is what your ITT tutors are actually asking you to do in writing assignments! If, at any time during your programme, you think this *is* what you are being asked to do, why not ask your tutor whether (or perhaps how) you can connect what you read to some aspect of practice (either observed or experienced), to help you understand its potential use and relevance?

There are a couple of other reasons we can think of that might make seeing the relevance of 'theory' difficult. First, many beginning teachers start their training by thinking there is 'one right way' of doing things that they need to learn how to do, and are frustrated at not being immediately taught how to 'do it'. If a person thinks like this, any 'theory' can seem irrelevant and a waste of time. Perhaps unfortunately though, as many of you reading may have discovered, there are many, many ways of helping people learn, and what's more we each have to discover and work out our own way. In fact, we have to work out our own *ways*, as there are so many different learners and contexts too. We can of course draw on the experience and guidance of more expert others, but in order to do a lot of this working out we need to have not only experience but also ways of planning for and explaining and understanding that experience (the 'theory'). In fact, many teachers, researchers and teachers of teachers (ToTs) would argue that, for someone to become an effective teacher, how they *think* about teaching and learning is just as important as what they *do*.

A second reason why it can be difficult for some trainees to see the relevance of theory is that some of the teachers and mentors in schools, with whom they (and you?) are working and from whom they (and perhaps you) are learning, are also sceptical about the value of the more theoretical work covered on some ITT courses, as the trainee quoted below suggests:

> In the opinion of people I've spoken to, the head teachers and teachers, you're never going to use it ['theory'], you need to have practical experience and confidence. That is my main objection to this course at the minute.
>
> (Male, 20–24, primary)

In some cases mentors have even been quoted as telling their trainees to 'forget about the theory and concentrate on the practice'!

The fact that some teachers and mentors think like this is also understandable. For example, some older teacher-mentors may be thinking back to the 'theory' they encountered in their own teacher training many moons ago, when the theory covered may indeed have been less relevant to the work of teachers than it is today. Second, mentors are first and foremost teachers (of pupils, not of student teachers) and as such may not have needed to put this kind of ('theoretical') thinking into words for many years, as the main practice of teaching does not require talking *about* teaching.

As we hope you are now beginning to recognise, however, learning to become an effective teacher *isn't* just a matter of being 'told' and 'shown' how to do it. Contexts (place, people and time) make *a big* difference, which means that some teaching methods and strategies may work for some pupils in some schools but not for other pupils in different schools or even other pupils in the same schools! Becoming an effective teacher thus requires you to develop skills of noticing (see Chapter 4) and ways of explaining and understanding what is noticed in order that you will be able eventually to make 'on the spot' judgments about what to do in different teaching situations. The 'theories' you are exposed to on your ITT course are intended to help you to do just that.

Here's one way you can use theories, and integrate them into your thinking to help your planning and/or the development of *your* way of thinking and teaching.[1] After some teaching (whether you were observing or teaching):

1 Describe what you noticed.
2 Take one intriguing/puzzling/problematic feature of your description and think of (and jot down) as many explanations as you can.
3 Now try to remember (go on, think back over recent sessions!) as many theories as you can, and see if any of those might help explain things (and add them to your list of possible explanations).
4 Decide which of the explanations on your list is most likely (you may need to use other information you have or other parts of your description to help in this).

5 So what? What were the likely impacts on pupils' learning of what you noticed if your explanation is right? What do the 'theories' you have encountered suggest might be needed next (for the pupils' or for your learning)? What will you (or might you expect the teacher to) do/plan for the next lesson? What more do you need to find out? What will you try to notice next time?

For example, you might notice three boys yawning, include this detail in your description of the lesson in question, and use it to start a five-step thinking process as above. You might then think (Step 2) that this could mean the boys were:

- tired;
- bored;
- deliberately 'playing up'; or
- digesting after lunch.

You might also wonder whether the room was too stuffy. At Step 3, you might remember hearing about some work done by Csikszentmihalyi (1990) which talked about emotions in relation to level of challenge being faced, and the skills available to meet the challenge. In this theory, boredom occurs when people have high-level skills but not enough challenge. On the other hand, 'flow' (a state of being so engrossed that people do not notice time passing) can be reached when the challenge is just right – that is, people are being stretched enough to keep things interesting, but have enough skills to cope. At Step 4 you would need to know and remember what time of day it was, what the room felt like, the tasks the boys were supposed to be engaged in and what you knew about the individuals themselves. If, for example, it was early in the day, there was enough air in the room and these were pupils who usually got high grades, you might conclude that it is most likely that the boys were in fact bored. Perhaps then at Step 5, and thinking of 'flow', you might decide that in future you (or the teacher) could differentiate the learning tasks more effectively so the boys (as well as their classmates) are appropriately 'stretched'.

The example we have used above to illustrate how the process might work uses just one small part of a description of a lesson – 'three boys yawned'. However, you could equally well use *patterns* you notice in the description you made – for example, 'I/the teacher called mostly on girls to answer questions'. The more that you notice, the richer your descriptions can be and the more potentially you should be able to learn from your experiences – and from those of others and from 'theory'!

You may recall that in Chapter 4 we explained that student teachers typically experience and seek to address a number of sequential concerns during their ITT, often starting with concerns about pupil behaviour and how to deal with it. If you have reached the stage of your ITT course and your development at which you feel you can 'cope', you are no longer panicking at the prospect of standing up in front of 30-odd boisterous children or teenagers, and you feel you have developed some basic classroom management skills, perhaps you might now be ready to think more about other kinds of 'theory'. On the other hand, even if you are only just starting your ITT course, it might nevertheless be helpful to start taking theory seriously *now*, not least because it can help you to plan and carry out interesting and engaging lessons, which will mean you are less likely to encounter pupil behaviour issues or find pupil behaviour troublesome in the first place.

It is worth remembering, as we pointed out in Chapter 3, that ITT course designers, planners and tutors have good reasons for including in their courses what they do. These may not *all* be directly related to your immediate practice of teaching, but many will, and all (including the qualification that you will hopefully achieve) will be relevant to the development of your future career. It is worth remembering too that your ITT tutors have usually been successful and experienced teachers themselves, and have been successful in introducing many other beginner teachers to the profession. So even if you have some doubts about some of the things they are telling you and asking you to do, it will tend to be in your best long-term interests to put your faith in them!

Theory as invisible influence

Finally, it is important (and perhaps reassuring) to know that even if you can't (or can't yet) recognise the relevance of theory or its influence on your work as a teacher, this does not mean that it isn't nevertheless influencing your thinking and 'practical' work – for it may be doing so without your conscious awareness. That is:

- Sometimes we're not sure why we make the decisions or follow the course of actions that we do; and
- It has been found that much good work goes on in our 'undermind' (Claxton, 1997) without us knowing about it, with our brains drawing on a huge amount of information gleaned from a range of experiences to help us to make (sometimes immediate) decisions.

One of the (moderately) theory-sceptical student teachers we spoke to entertained such a possibility:

> I feel that things like learning about theories of how children learn and things are useful, but I can't honestly say I've ever put them in my teaching . . . Maybe I do subconsciously but I don't know. I think it will probably become more useful.
>
> (Female, 20–24, secondary)

Conclusion

In Chapters 5 and 6 we have discussed two major issues (pupil behaviour and the relevance of course theory) that influence the quality of your ITT experience and the extent of your learning as a beginner teacher. In Chapter 7 we deal with another, and the thing that makes the human world go around . . . *relationships*!

Chapter 7

'I'm glad I've built up such good relationships'

Building and maintaining productive relationships in ITT

Introduction

We saw in Chapters 1 and 2 that many people are attracted to teaching, and to particular ITT routes, by the prospect of working and enjoying meaningful relationships with other people. For example, 92 per cent of respondents to our survey said they were attracted to teaching by the idea of 'working with children or young people', and 57 per cent by 'the collegiality/teamwork aspects of teaching', while 34 per cent of respondents (and 43 per cent of those choosing to follow PGCE programmes) said that one of the factors influencing their choice of ITT route was the desire to 'train alongside people in my peer group/in the same situation' as themselves. In addition, 84 per cent of respondents said that before they began their ITT programmes they were 'particularly looking forward' to 'being in classrooms and interacting with children', and 45 per cent said they were 'particularly looking forward' to 'becoming a part of the school community'.

Were these potential benefits amongst the reasons *you* wanted to become a teacher or follow a particular ITT route? And, for those of you presently following an ITT course, are you actually experiencing these potential benefits? Or are you encountering some problems in getting on with people on your course or in your school, as is often the case?

If you are now part-way through your ITT course, you will recognise that the extent to which you feel 'up' or 'down' about your ITT will largely be determined by how well you are getting along with pupils and teachers in your placement schools, as well as other people (e.g. university tutors) associated with your course. You might also recognise and appreciate the value of maintaining good relations with your peers (other student teachers) and your friends and family.

This chapter emphasises the importance, in navigating your ITT course, of developing and maintaining productive relationships with both children and adults, and (building on suggestions for forming productive relationships given in Chapter 3) suggests a number of strategies to help maintain and sustain relationships, including ways of resolving interpersonal conflicts.

Are relationships important in ITT?

What do you think? Which relationships do you think are most important? And which ones do you find easiest and most difficult to maintain?

Our research shows that the extent to which student teachers feel positive about their ITT is largely dependent upon how well they are getting on with a range of 'significant others' associated with their courses, especially the pupils they are teaching and the mentors and other teacher colleagues in their placement schools. Relationships are particularly important in ITT because they are central to the activities in which you are primarily engaged as a student teacher, namely teaching and learning. First, for example, you will need to demonstrate, during your ITT, that you are capable of helping pupils to learn, and this is difficult to achieve if you are not able to establish and maintain productive working relationships with them. Second, mentors and other teachers in school are key resources who can help you to develop your own learning to become a teacher. The more productive your relationships with them, the more you are likely to learn and the more successful you are likely to be.

Which relationships are most important?

It will be beneficial to you if, during your ITT, you are able to develop and maintain good relationships with a whole range of people, including university-based tutors (if you have them), and head teachers, teaching assistants and pupils' parents in your placement schools. However, in our experience, and according to our research, relationships with five different groups of people are especially important. We discuss each of these below.

1 Relationships with pupils

First, it is important to student teachers, and to their enjoyment of ITT and teaching, that they get on with the pupils they teach. A trainee we quoted in Chapter 5 found teaching enjoyable and the children 'really nice and very sociable and friendly'. Another trainee defined whether or not a period in schools had been successful by her relationships with the children:

> [A] good teaching practice was where I responded well to the children and built good relationships with them.
>
> (Female, 20–24, primary)

How would you rate your relationships with the pupils you teach, and how might you be able to improve these?

2 Relationships with mentors

Second, many of the trainees in our research spoke about how their relationships with their mentors had had a positive impact on their experiences of ITT. Some of these talked about the specific ways in which their mentors had helped them, including boosting their confidence and making them 'feel valued', providing strategies and/or support for classroom management, 'being there/available', and offering guidance for managing time and workload. One student teacher echoed the sentiments of many in saying that 'My mentor has probably been the most influential person [in my training]'.

However, other student teachers were not so lucky, and many trainees in our research said they did not have good relationships with their mentors for a variety of reasons, including mentors being unsupportive, 'too busy' or 'too critical', as illustrated in the following quotations.

> The teacher used to come in at about half past eight and leave at half past three, so I didn't really get much support from her at all . . . I think it was two weeks into my placement and I thought I really can't do this because obviously I wasn't getting the support and I was in floods of tears.
>
> (Female, 25–29, primary)

> [I]t was a really oppressive atmosphere in the school. Off my actual mentor . . . I got nothing but criticism and pressure from her from day one. She was criticising everything I did . . . I mean we had been doing a lot on the course on the power of positive feedback . . . and I got none whatsoever.
>
> (Male, 25–29, secondary)

In addition, we saw in Chapter 4 that some mentors were reluctant to 'let go' of their classes and to let trainees take on responsibilities that would facilitate their learning, and at least one of the trainees in our research felt that her mentor treated her more like a 'dogsbody' than a learner-teacher. Some suggestions for dealing with those kinds of experiences were provided in Chapter 4.

So do you enjoy a good, productive relationship with your mentor? Do you feel that you are treated appropriately by your mentor? If the answer to either of these questions is 'no', is there anything you could do about it?

3 Relationships with other teachers

It is also helpful, for various reasons, if you get on with other teacher colleagues in your placement schools. As one of the student teachers in our research put it:

> I'm very glad that I've built up such good relationships with the other staff really because otherwise I would have felt quite isolated, I think.
>
> (Female, 25–29, secondary)

Establishing good relationships with a range of teacher colleagues becomes particularly important in situations where you perceive your mentor to be unsupportive. Some trainees in our research who reported dysfunctional relationships with mentors said they had been 'saved' by relationships they had established with other teachers in their placement schools:

> In my placement my class teacher [and mentor] wasn't so great, but the deputy head and a teacher that I had got quite friendly with from Year 1, she was absolutely fantastic and she went through all the planning with me and, because I really did, in my first week, I really did want to throw in the towel and think I'd had enough because I wasn't getting the support.
>
> (Female, 25–29, primary)

So it might help to think of mentoring as potentially coming from more than one person – a kind of 'dispersed mentoring'. If your mentor doesn't (or can't for whatever reason) provide you with emotional support, for example, think about who in the school (or outside) can. If you mentor doesn't model being the kind of teacher you aspire to becoming, can you find another who does? If your mentor doesn't help you learn how to learn from your experiences, can you get help from elsewhere? You get the idea! One task during an observation period might be, as Oberski *et al.* (1999) recommend, to make a profile of your new school, focusing on relationships within it to understand its culture and identify potential future sources of support.

Once you have identified what it is that you ideally want or need from your mentor that he or she cannot or does not provide (and perhaps after having the kind of 'understanding talk' we recommended in Chapter 4), be proactive – take charge of your own learning and use the many resources available to you during your ITT course to get what you need.

More generally it will be beneficial if, during your ITT placements, you can become part of a team. Many of the student teachers in our research provided indications that their experiences were more or less positive according to the extent to which they felt that their school-based experiences had been characterised by collaboration, cooperation and teamwork. Although some teachers will be more ready to accept you into their teams than others, there are things that you can do to try to encourage this, as we suggest below.

4 Relationships with your peers

Some student teachers in our research also highlighted the importance of relationships with, or the presence of, fellow trainees in relation to their school-based experiences, as illustrated in the following quotation:

> The programme that the school created for us, nine PGCE students in the school, two in the maths department which is great, having somebody else there in the department is really good . . . really good.
> (Male, 40–44, secondary)

The presence of other trainees in the school, and having good relationships with such people, is especially important in a situation in which you do not feel welcome in your placement schools, which can sometimes be the case, as illustrated in the following quotation:

> [N]one of the other teachers would talk to us and there were five students there, so we were always sticking together but we were in different subjects in five different departments. In general we were shunned in the staffroom . . . If I was on my own I would find this quite an isolating experience.
> (Female, 25–29, secondary)

Are you making the most of your fellow trainees? Or are you spending *too much* time with them, perhaps because it feels safe and is easier than taking advantage of opportunities to build relationships with established members of staff?

5 Relationships with friends and family

Maintaining good relationships with partners, friends and family members is also very important during your ITT. On the one hand, such people can be extremely valuable in providing emotional and practical support during what can be a difficult and stressful period.

> [M]y husband is extremely supportive and he has been really very helpful and I would say that without his support it would have been

difficult . . . Because it is a difficult thing to do when you have got a family and you have got a home . . . there is so much to do. The children must have clothes to wear, you know, they must have food to eat and somebody has got to do that.

(Female, 35–39, primary)

On the other hand, the stresses and strains of following an ITT course can potentially impact detrimentally on your relationships with family and friends, and cause problems with personal relationships, which can then be a source of further stress. Many student teachers we talked to said that they had 'no life' during their ITT, and some, such as the trainee we quote below, told us about the impact on their personal and family lives:

We [trainee and her husband] have found it very stressful . . . There have been times when we've barely spoken to each other to be honest. We just get to the point where you're too tired and you can't do anything. You don't want to go out and that does have repercussions on your relationship. We've had some fraught times. My daughter is in [location] and I've never managed to get down to see her or anything. A weekend to go down to [see her] was impossible. Too much work to do.

(Female, 45 or over, secondary)

Another trainee, whom we quoted in Chapter 4, talked about 'the guilt' related to her feeling that she had 'probably given teacher training more than I have given my family'.

Are *you* neglecting your relationships with family and friends, or putting your ITT before your loved ones? If you are, what are you going to do about it? (Again, some ideas on dealing with such scenarios are discussed in Chapter 4.)

Developing and maintaining productive relationships

So it is important that you attempt to form and maintain productive educational relationships. How might you do this?

The basis of any good relationship is mutual trust

It will, for example, be vital to *earn* the trust of the children. They need to trust that you are a good person to support their learning and that you are able to create the conditions for this to happen and keep them 'safe' as they do so. And trust needs to be mutual – they also need to know you trust them. So how far do you genuinely trust that the children in your charge are capable of learning and behaving appropriately and want to do both these things? (Back to the need for positive expectations again!)

Your mentors and colleagues will need to trust that you are as concerned as them for the pupils' welfare and learning and that, partly in consequence, you are there to learn from and with them. You need to trust that your mentor and colleagues are in the best position, and are willing and able, to help you learn classroom teaching and to become a member of the school and broader professional communities.

Your family and friends need to trust that you care about them enough to safeguard some time for your relationships with them even in this very busy period, and you need to trust that your family and friends understand that, although you may be spending less time with them than before, this is probably temporary and does not indicate that you love them any less.

What trusting and demonstrating trustworthiness requires

Trusting and being trustworthy requires transparency or openness and communication. But we learn to trust (or mistrust) someone as much by what they do (or don't do) as by what they say, so open honest communication, though necessary, will not be enough. It will need to be matched by actions and behaviour. All of this requires time – time for talk and time for actions matching talk, which provide evidence of trustworthiness, engender trust, and lead to the development of good relationships.

With regard to *pre-existing* relationships, perhaps the most important is your relationship with yourself! We have already suggested (in Chapter 4) that making time for yourself might become a 'big rock' in your weekly planning. You could also think in such terms about time for and with your family. Recognising the impact that following the ITT course was having on her personal and family life, the trainee we quoted above, who rarely went out and who had 'some fraught times' with her husband, talked about one of the strategies she adopted for restoring some balance to her life:

> I made a vow though after Christmas, that I am just not going to let that happen. This term we've made a point of, on a Saturday, regardless of housework, we got out, go to the country and go for a walk.
>
> (Female, 45 or over, secondary)

If you find yourself with fellow trainees in schools, they may or may not be people you already know, but you can probably trust each other to understand and empathise with the struggles and emotional impacts of your common endeavour – if you are open and talk about it.

With regard to your *new* relationships, those with pupils are central. One way of seeing the development of these is that they require, as a starting point, good class management, and in Chapter 5 we discuss the necessity to 'start right' and 'practise what you preach'. Much of what we wrote there – about making rules clear and being consistent, for example – could be seen from the perspective of earning trust and demonstrating trustworthiness. Of course when you have built good productive relationships with individual pupils or classes, and earned their trust, and they yours, class management becomes much easier – you will not constantly be tested to see if you meant what you said or to see if you are trustworthy, for example, as they will know that you did/are.

For all ITT mentors (although not all will show or feel it as keenly as the mentor we have referred to who did not want to 'let go' of her class), it is already an act of trust in you to hand over to you some or all of the teaching of pupils for whom they have responsibility and for whose learning and welfare they are held accountable. As we are sure you realise, you can repay that trust best by being trustworthy: punctual, prepared, committed, actively learning – and all those professional qualities that committed teachers display. On the other hand, as we suggested earlier, the mentor needs to earn *your* trust too: by virtue of their position, in most systems, they are the person most responsible for supporting your learning when you are in their school, and you need to know by their actions and words that they are able and willing to do so.

The other teachers in the school need to trust that you will respect them and their experience (even if you do bring new or different ideas), that you want to join with them in the whole school endeavour of educating its pupils and that you see in them the source of much of the wisdom of the profession. Again, you also need to trust: that they will welcome you into the school and the profession; that they will, if asked, do what they can to support your learning; and that they will be interested in the ideas and experience you bring.

Our research found that older entrants to the teaching profession sometimes had more difficulties establishing good relationships with mentors and other teacher colleagues than younger ones. For example, 52 per cent of those trainees aged 25–34 rated their relationships with their mentors as 'very good', compared with 42 per cent of those aged 45 or over, of whom 8 per cent reported 'poor' or 'very poor' relations. Difficulties of establishing positive relationships with mentors and other colleagues seemed to many of these research participants to result from a perception that previous work and life experiences suddenly 'count for nothing' in the eyes of these new colleagues. If you are in this category and find yourself thinking like this, perhaps you could ask yourself who is not trusting whom (in the sense described above)? And given that 'you can't change other people, you can only change yourself', one thing you might consider is what more *you* could do to demonstrate trustworthiness. Conversations of the kind described in Chapter 4 might also help: 'I know I might *look* like more established teachers and behave with more self-assurance because I'm older than the trainees you have been used to having, but I am a novice at this and I really need and would value your help. In return, if you like, I have had some experience (in management, or whatever it is) which I'd be happy to share at any time, if it would be helpful.'

Maintaining good relationships and resolving interpersonal conflicts

The key to maintaining good relationships is again spending time together, continuing open communication and developing and deepening trust. It is also valuing the relationship sufficiently to take the trouble to talk over and try to resolve any interpersonal conflicts that arise. As we said in Chapter 4, conversations such as these need to be planned, and the time and place agreed beforehand.

As we are human, and all of us still learning, so all relationships (however well they may begin and however sound they are in general) go through rocky patches. These may be due to breaches of trust, or a lack of openness in the first place or, conversely (because of increased trust and a consequent increased openness), the discovery of seemingly irreconcilable differences. The good news is that, if we can resolve these interpersonal conflicts, the relationship can be all the stronger for having had (and having resolved) the conflict.

Whereas in our broader lives if relationships (with friends, for example) become difficult we can choose to end them, this is often not a practical option in our professional lives. As a trainee, it will be important (as we saw above) to build and maintain good relationships with a range of people. You will, in any case, be potentially spending as much if not more time with the people in schools than with your friends and family, which, in terms of professional relationship maintenance, is a good thing. But are there colleagues with whom you could, and perhaps should, spend time but you don't? Have you been less than trustworthy or appropriately open at times?

In what follows we describe some 'tools for thinking' that have helped the authors in thinking through and talking through the kind of interpersonal conflicts that can arise as we try to maintain good professional relationships.

First, a tutor once told us that any conflicts between people are as a result of differences in one or more of the three 'i's: *information, interests* and *ideology*. If people have different *information*, or one knows more than the other, and neither perhaps is aware of what the other knows, this can cause miscommunication and conflicts. So the first step in a conflict might be to check out what each other knows or understands and, if necessary, 'fill each other in'. A conflict-resolving talk (almost always desirable in adult–adult conflicts) might begin, for example, with 'Let's just check we both understand the same thing here.' If a lack of shared information was the problem it is relatively easily solved – but again, and crucially, will require both parties to value the relationship enough to talk about the problem and sort it out.

Some relationship problems, though, result from the second 'i' – people having different *interests* or goals. For example, your teenage pupils' goals may include impressing classmates, whereas your primary goal is to get them to engage in activity that will support their learning. Or a designated mentor's primary goal might be to ensure that her pupils do well in their forthcoming examinations, whereas yours, as a trainee, will be to learn to teach. The trick here is first of all to recognise the different interests. Whereas with the adults in school you may be able to find out what their primary goals are through talk (although not everyone is necessarily very self-aware), usually with pupils you will need to gain an understanding of their primary goals more through your professional reading and interactions than through asking them, as they are less likely to be able – or even willing – to articulate this. Once the interests of the different parties are clear or out in the open, it becomes easier to discover ways in which both parties can achieve their goals. With regard to your pupils, perhaps you can find a way of getting the (unofficial) 'group leader' in the class, the one that everyone wants to be seen with and impress, on your side (maybe by giving them some responsibility or leading an after-school club in which they shine), so that engaging in productive learning activity (your goal) will also enable the other pupils to impress classmates (their goal). With regard to the 'reluctant mentor', perhaps you could suggest that she (or he) always talk you carefully through her (or his) plans for the class and then stage the process by which you take on more responsibility. For example, after modelling how she realises her plans in her class for a few lessons, and when she is confident you understand what, how and why she does things as she does, she might let you take over some of the teaching, and then more and more of the teaching, and then the planning as well as the teaching, as she becomes more confident in you. In this way both of you can achieve your goals. The aim, when a conflict of interests has been established, is to get to a win–win situation.

Differences in *ideology* or in fundamental beliefs (the third 'i') are much more difficult not only to unearth but also to reconcile. If you discover these (e.g. one of you believing, or acting as if you believe, that children are essentially 'naughty' and need to have goodness trained into them, whereas the other believes that children are essentially good and want to 'behave' and learn, and that unacceptable behaviour is a way of signalling unhelpful conditions for learning somewhere in their lives or simply a learning adulthood mistake), you may have to agree to disagree. It will, however, be a valuable opportunity for you to think carefully about what it is you *do* believe.

Second, the theory of 'basic psychological needs' (BPN), which we discussed briefly in Chapter 5 in the context of understanding pupil behaviour, is helpful in trying to understand the reason behind the words or actions which may have upset us, or the 'interests' they were intended to serve. Whereas with pupils an idea of what basic need the pupil was trying to meet through his or her words or actions can help us decide on strategies to use, with adults in school it can help in formulating a possible opening line of a conflict-resolving conversation, in which it will be important that you try your best to show that you are working on understanding the other. (If you don't attempt to understand them, why should they attempt to understand you?)

In sum, one way to approach conflict situations is to:

- talk about it;
- bear in mind the three 'i's and basic psychological needs; and
- believe you can find a way to resolve things and aim for that outcome.

Building and maintaining group relationships

When we are thinking about building and maintaining relationships in the contexts of groups – e.g. pupil class groups or teams of colleagues – we have found insights from *group dynamics* helpful. This area of study has taught us that groups and teams go through predictable phases of group life, and the most memorable way of expressing these we have found is: 'forming, norming, storming, performing and mourning' (Argyle, 1969; Heron, 1989).

In the *forming* phase, three things are important:

1   establishing inter-member relationships (everyone learning names and finding out about each other);
2   establishing group norms and ways of working;
3   establishing shared goals.

So, have you learnt your pupils' and colleagues' names? Do you know something about all of them? Have you let them know something about you? Have you established clearly (or negotiated) the 'class rules' (see Chapter 5) for each group you teach? Are these made explicit in each of the working groups or teams you belong to? You will doubtless have let your pupils know about the syllabus, but have you asked them what, within that, they most want to learn? Can you make the learning goals more 'shared' rather than simply top-down and imposed by you? (Perhaps not during your training, but this is something to think about for later.) What about the goals of the teams you belong to? Have these been made explicit and are they 'shared'?

The second phase of group life is the *norming* phase, one in which people get used to behaving according to the rules. Then comes the *storming* phase. This is predictable, remember, and not 'your fault' – when group members become comfortable enough for differences and conflicts to become apparent. And this is when all your conflict resolution skills will be most needed (and possibly goals and rules renegotiated), as only when this phase is safely navigated can the crucial *performing* phase be reached – the one in which the group finally starts effectively achieving what is was formed to achieve (e.g. learning, in the case of class groups, or producing materials or plans for a team of colleagues). Last, if the collection of individuals has in fact been a 'group' in this psycho-social sense, there will be a *mourning* phase in which people will be genuinely sad that the experience is over. There are three important things to do in this phase too (if people are to feel motivated to engage in similar teams or groups in the future). These are:

1   to review the experience – remembering key moments and how they felt, for example;
2   to review, acknowledge and celebrate the learning and achievements – as important for teacher teams as for more intentional learning groups such as classes of pupils;
3   to ensure that all group members have what they need to continue their work/learning without the support of the group.

We have found that sometimes thinking in terms of group dynamics about what is happening in the groups we lead (our classes) or teams we belong to has helped us in our quest to form and maintain those all-important professional relationships with pupils and colleagues.[1]

Finally, as always, if you are having problems in your relationships with any of the people we discuss in this chapter, and you are finding it difficult to resolve these, talk to your mentor and/or course tutors. Don't hide or bury your head in the sand – relationships are at the heart of learning and education so we should always do our best to make them work!

Conclusion

In this chapter we have revisited one of the recurring themes in the experiences of the student teachers we talked to in our research – that of the importance to them, and to their experience of ITT, of creating and maintaining good relationships. We have suggested some ways (such as self-disclosing, demonstrating trustworthiness, devoting time and talking about the relationship) that might help you create and maintain good relationships with a range of people involved in or affected by your decision to undertake an ITT programme. We have also provided some strategies for thinking about, and so possibly resolving or minimising, any interpersonal conflicts you may experience. In the next chapter we discuss issues that cause some people to consider withdrawing from their ITT programmes.

Chapter 8

'I can't be doing with it'

Are you thinking of quitting ITT?

Introduction

In this chapter we discuss the issues that cause some people to make the decision not to complete the ITT programmes they start. For those readers who may be encountering similar problems, we offer a number of strategies for dealing both with the specific problems you are experiencing and with the difficult decision about whether or not to withdraw. If you are experiencing problems on your ITT course and have begun to consider whether or not you can or should complete your course, the first thing we would say is that this is not an unusual experience – many student teachers feel like this on at least some occasions. The second point we would make to those in this situation is that there are a range of options available to you. These include:

- rethinking the nature of your experience, which might lead you to conclude that the issues you are facing are not as problematic or serious as you first thought;
- attempting to resolve any very real problems that you are experiencing;
- deciding that the problems you are experiencing are beyond resolution.

   More specifically, in terms of outcomes, your options include:

- deciding to withdraw from your ITT course and giving up on the idea of teaching as a career;
- deciding to withdraw from ITT but leaving open the possibility of returning to ITT at some point in the future;
- deferring completion of your ITT course;
- attempting to successfully complete your ITT with little or no intention of subsequently taking up a teaching post;
- attempting to successfully complete your ITT and persevering with the idea of becoming a teacher.

If you are experiencing problems, we hope that by the end of this chapter you will be a little clearer about which of these potential courses of action and outcomes might be most appropriate for *you*.

Why do some people withdraw from or defer completion of ITT?

In our survey of 3,162 people who were completing or had been due to complete ITT programmes in England, 135 told us that they had withdrawn from their programmes and 45 told us that they had deferred completion of their ITT. The main substantive reasons given by those who *withdrew* from their ITT programmes were as follows:

- a perceived inability to manage the workload (22 per cent said this had been a contributory factor in causing them to drop out);
- a perceived lack of appropriate support (15 per cent);
- family reasons/commitments (10 per cent);
- ill health (8 per cent);
- poor pupil behaviour (8 per cent);
- found teaching too difficult (6 per cent);
- found training too difficult (5 per cent).

Some respondents gave the somewhat less specific response that they had 'changed their minds' about teaching as a career, 12 per cent said they were not enjoying their school placements, 8 per cent said they were not enjoying the teaching and another 8 per cent said they were not enjoying the training. These responses (the reasons they were not enjoying ITT and changed their minds about becoming teachers) can probably be attributed in large measure to one or more of the other factors listed above.

We also asked those survey respondents who had withdrawn from their ITT programmes what might have prevented them from withdrawing. The main responses were as follows:

- more support from their ITT provider (19 per cent);
- more support from their school mentor(s) (19 per cent);
- a more manageable workload (17 per cent);
- placement at different school(s) (9 per cent);
- better respect/discipline of the pupils (5 per cent);
- financial assistance (4 per cent);
- nothing (11 per cent).

From these different questions we see that 'the usual suspects' of workload and a perceived lack of support, followed by other issues including pupil discipline, were the major problems contributing to student teacher withdrawal. Those respondents who had *deferred completion* of their ITT, on the other hand, attributed their decision predominantly to family reasons or commitments (29 per cent) and ill health (27 per cent), though 9 per cent also indicated that they could not cope with the workload.

Are any of these (or other) factors causing you to have serious reservations about continuing on your ITT programme? If they are, have you considered or tried out any of the ideas in this book as a means of potentially rethinking, resolving or minimising the problems you are experiencing?

In what follows we discuss in more detail the major issues causing people to withdraw from or defer completion of their courses, and offer further suggestions or reminders for how you might address them. In doing so we draw on the conversations we had with six ex-trainees who had either withdrawn from or deferred completion of their ITT. By giving some insights into their experiences and the extent to which some of the issues affected them, this might help you to put your own experiences into perspective. But, as we said above, and to repeat, if you feel you may be in danger of approaching the stage where you are considering whether you can continue with your ITT: (1) talk to someone (or several people); and (2) *do* something about addressing and resolving the problem(s) you are experiencing as soon as possible, before it all becomes just too much. This issue is illustrated in the following quotation from an ex-trainee who *did* leave it too late:

> I think, with working in industry previously, if there is a problem, you tend to get on with it, don't you, you don't just run back to your tutor and say I really can't cope and in retrospect I should have done . . . At the time when I couldn't really cope, it was too late for me personally to rectify the situation . . . And when it gets to that stage the only way to go really is to say 'I am not cut out for this'.
>
> (Female, 25–29, secondary)

We do not know enough about whether and to what extent the trainees whose words we cite next had had access to, or tried to act on, the kinds of suggestions we make in this book. If they had, perhaps some of them might be teaching now. So, to reiterate, this next section is not intended to deepen your gloom, but rather to help you identify and see clearly the possible causes of your concerns and help you make the best decision for you. The first step to solving a problem is to see it clearly, to understand it and to name it.

1 Workload and work–life balance

For some (ex-)trainees that we spoke to, twin responsibilities relating to work and to home life proved too difficult for them to manage. This was the case for the ex-trainee we quote below, whose decision to leave was clearly also influenced by a number of additional considerations including pay:

> [I]f I'd been doing the training course 10 years ago before I had any children, I don't think it would've been such an issue and I would've just completed it. I think the realisation came to me that I was studying for a qualification that would allow me to do a job where I had very little respect, I would be taking a huge drop in salary and yet I was actually working harder than I would work in another profession. So I got another job . . . for better pay and I could have a better family/life balance.
>
> (Female, 40–44, secondary)

Another ex-trainee talked about how her experience of following an ITT programme impacted detrimentally not only on her work–life balance but also on her health. Again, she found it impossible to combine school work, college work and domestic responsibilities, saying that she had 'never worked so hard trying to balance everything out' and that she had 'no time for a social life'. She felt she had to make a choice between her husband and family and her ambition to be a teacher:

> What the course has done to me has made me realise how important my family are regardless of whatever job I'm going to do.
>
> (Female, 40–44, primary)

Reflecting on some of the pros and cons of teaching as a career, one (ex-)trainee explained how her issues with the workload and the 'administrative' aspects of teaching eventually forced her hand:

> I love working with the kids, it is superb, but it is all the extra stuff, all the hassle. I can't be doing with it. I would rather have a boring nine to five job, I would hate it, but I would prefer that to having to work 70–80 hours a week, which is what I have been doing. Something has to give.
>
> (Female, 20–24, secondary)

How does *your* experience compare with those of the ex-trainees cited above? If you had previously thought that workload management was a problem for you, do you still think so? If so, have you talked to others about how they manage? Have you tried to implement any of the strategies suggested on your ITT programme, or any of those suggested in this book?

Perhaps part of the explanation for *your* workload issues is that you are striving to be perfect? If so, read on. It might help to know that the pupils will appreciate and learn from a teacher who is alert and prepared and eager to interact with them (even if every 'i' is not dotted on the plan and the materials are not quite as polished as they might be). In fact, they will probably learn from such a teacher better than from a teacher with perfect plans and materials that took half the night to prepare and who is, as a result, both exhausted and 'over-planned', which makes it less likely that they will notice or respond appropriately to the actual responses of pupils! And the disappointing lesson that then ensues – despite all the hard work – can prompt, in some, the belief that they need to work even harder, leading to more exhaustion for the teacher and even more diminished ability to respond . . . a vicious cycle. Is this you? Do you recognise a perfectionist streak in yourself? If you're feeling like quitting and workload is your main reason, we suggest that you 'give yourself a break' – literally *and* metaphorically (you're still *learning* teaching after all, and could try being as patient with yourself as you need to be with your learners!). We are reminded of a story we read about Ghandi:

> Ghandi was a busy man but he always meditated for two hours every day. People marvelled at how he could afford the time given everything else he had to do. One man even asked him what he did about his meditation when he was really busy. Ghandi replied: 'When I'm really busy? Oh, well, then I meditate for three hours a day.'[1]

So however hard it may seem, and however 'unjustified' it may feel (given all there is that you have not done/need to do), take that break! Then, decide how much time you can afford to give to each of the tasks that need doing and stick to it. And remember to plan in that 'big rock' called 'self' too (see Chapter 4) – as Ghandi recognised, time for your self is even more important when you are really busy.

2 Lack of support

Like some of the survey respondents referred to above, some of the ex-trainees we spoke to talked about a lack of appropriate support from their mentors and other teachers in their placement schools as major factors in their decisions to withdraw from or defer completion of their ITT. A lack of support can take many guises. For example, you might feel that your mentor and/or other teachers and tutors associated with your ITT programme are not making sufficient time for you, are not helping you with specific issues with which you need help, are not sufficiently welcoming or encouraging, or are too negative in their 'constructive criticism' of your planning and/or teaching attempts. In addition to the quotation provided in the last chapter from the ex-trainee who talked about getting 'nothing but criticism and pressure' from his mentor 'from day one', the following quotations from other ex-trainees we spoke to illustrate some of these issues:

> They're busy, every teacher's busy, and to have a new student [teacher] in it takes a lot and sometimes I felt they didn't give me enough time.
>
> (Female, 40–44, primary)

> We missed a lot of [planned] mentor sessions as well at school B, which didn't help.
>
> (Male, 30–34, secondary)

> I thought they [the teachers] were amazingly unsupportive if I'm absolutely truthful. I think they were truly horrible . . . You just got the feeling you weren't allowed to say anything . . . I wanted to engage in it [teaching] and talk about it and of course, a lot of teachers just want you to shut up.
>
> (Female, 40–44, secondary)

One ex-trainee said that she had expressed concern to her mentor about her lack of subject knowledge relating to a topic she had been asked to teach in her placement school, but that he provided no constructive help beyond 'you need to read up about it'. And some ex-trainees who were following HEI-administered programmes felt that there was a lack of appropriate support from their HEI-based tutors for problems they were experiencing in their placement schools:

> When I was having problems with my first school, he [HEI-based tutor] said, 'Well it is obviously a personality clash and other people have had perfectly successful practices there [in the same school],' which was blaming me, which was the last thing I needed.
>
> (Female, 20–24, secondary)

> I just kept getting told that this mentor was the best mentor they have got . . . so I think that doesn't help me.
>
> (Male, 30–34, secondary)

> I would have liked my tutor to have actually listened to me . . . she didn't really take it as seriously as she should have done.
>
> (Female, 25–29, secondary)

In addition to feeling that insufficient or inappropriate support had been offered to them by ITT programme personnel, three ex-trainee interviewees said they had been reluctant to approach anyone associated with their ITT programme to ask for advice, largely because of their awareness of how busy these people were.

If you count 'lack of support' among the reasons why *you* are thinking of withdrawing, have you actually asked for the support you need? The teachers of teachers (ToTs) associated with your ITT programme *may* be able to help you but may not presently be aware that you need help. You might have to make the first move! And if the person you would normally ask or expect support from (for example, your mentor) is unable (for whatever reason) to provide that support, have you considered the idea of 'dispersed mentoring' we suggested in Chapter 7 – in which a small group of different people each provide you with some of the support you need? Or have you explored other potential sources of support? In fact, different ITT programmes, or the institutions in which they are based, will usually have a number of support mechanisms that you might potentially access, including:

- a personal tutor;
- academic support;
- a counselling service;
- financial assistance;
- systems designed to help trainees experiencing problems to postpone their studies and return to ITT at a later date, where appropriate.

Are any of these potential forms of support available to you? If you are not sure, where might you be able to find out? A good place to start is usually your ITT course handbook.

On the other hand, you might prefer to draw on an existing support network away from your ITT programme – for example, amongst your family or friends – or you *could* form a new one, perhaps amongst fellow trainees, as the ex-trainee we quote below regretted *not* doing:

> [W]e didn't as a group get together . . . I went into university last week, and they [other students] were saying the same things, that they should have got together more because they were feeling bad, but not until I told everybody did I get e-mails back saying 'yes, I've been having some trouble' . . . and you wouldn't know that they had been in trouble and we haven't been helping each other. We haven't built up enough of a support group.
>
> (Male, 40–44, secondary)

When you have done your research, you could draw up a list of possible sources of assistance and *seek help* from the people who seem most likely to be able to help, *even if you think they are very busy* (it is their job to help you). If the first people you approach are not able to help, go to the next person on your list. And remember that no-one (well, no-one who really understands what it takes to become a teacher) will think the worse of you if you do ask for help/support – quite the contrary, as it shows that you are prepared to take charge of your own learning. This, in turn, can be seen as indicating that you could become a *really* good teacher, as there is a sense in which it is only when we can manage our own learning that we can effectively manage that of others.

Problems relating to a perceived lack of support are often related to relationship issues we discussed in the last chapter. If this is the case for you, have you tried some or all of the suggestions we made there for building and sustaining productive relationships? More specifically, for those of you who are unhappy about what you see as unduly negative critical commentary (e.g. from your mentor), it might be worth remembering that this will normally come from a genuine concern to help you succeed. Perhaps you could try to understand that the comments are not made about you as a person, just about your early attempts at teaching or an aspect of teaching, such as planning, which, inevitably (since you are not yet a qualified teacher) you won't yet have mastered! It may well be that the mentor, teacher or tutor concerned could have been more sensitive about how they had spoken to you, but they might be having problems themselves that you're not aware of, and it might be more productive for you to focus your energies not on their lack of sensitivity but on ways of developing the knowledge or skills in question. If you find your feelings get in the way of this, you could try an interpersonal conflict resolution conversation (see Chapter 7) that you might begin by saying something like: 'I realise you are trying to help me learn by pointing out the mistakes I am making, but . . .' and express how you feel and the kind of help that you would really appreciate.

As always, our suggestions are 'talk about it' and 'do something about it'!

3 Pupil behaviour and discipline

If you are tearing your hair out over pupil behaviour, have you asked for specific help with this? Have you read about and tried some of the strategies we suggest in Chapter 5? If so, have you given them time to work? Sometimes if you haven't used appropriate behaviour management techniques from the start you can 'lose' the group and it can be difficult to get them back or to get them to where you would like them to be. Resolve to 'start right' next time. During ITT, you will find yourself 'starting' again in no time!

4 Finding teaching and/or training difficult

Some trainees found that they had in fact held unrealistic expectations about themselves or how much work there would be during ITT:

Ultimately, teaching could be a fantastic job . . . and it wasn't that I was really awful at it or anything like that, I just felt, blimey, in terms of input and stuff, then this was one of the hardest jobs I ever tried.

(Female, 40–44, secondary)

It suddenly hits you halfway through the first block [school placement], you are not going to be as good a teacher as you thought you were going to be, because there is so much to do . . . And it just isn't doable, and it gets really demoralising.

(Male, 40–44, secondary)

People outside the profession rarely understand just how much learning is involved in becoming a teacher. If you have begun to realise and are somewhat daunted by what it takes, you can take comfort from the fact that at least you have learnt what it is you need to learn – and that is an important first step towards working out how to proceed or whether you have (or can give) what it takes!

5 Family commitments

The impact of family commitments on student teachers' experience of ITT is often associated with the high workload involved, which we discussed above. But there are some additional considerations and additional points we would like to make.

Those case study trainees who withdrew from or deferred completion of their ITT all indicated that their personal lives had had an impact on their ITT and that this could be something of a mixed blessing. On the one hand, family responsibilities can help trainees maintain some perspective on the place of ITT within their lives. On the other hand, this can simply add to their guilt if (as all six of our interviewees who withdrew from or deferred completion of their ITT appear to have done to some extent) they put their ITT before their loved ones in order to be able to deal with the pressures of their course.

If you are in the position where you can see that your ITT is having a detrimental effect on your family or personal life, but have not yet reached the stage where you are ready to decide whether or not you should withdraw or defer because of this, in Chapter 7 and in this chapter we discuss some strategies you could try to help alleviate the situation, or help you to make an informed decision.

6 Financial problems

Older trainees, in particular, who withdrew from or deferred completion of their ITT often cited financial problems among the reasons for their decision. Again we would suggest, as with most other issues, that you first talk to people. Family members, programme leaders and bank managers are some of the people who might be able to make helpful suggestions.

7 Ill health

Sometimes the flare-up of a pre-existing health condition, or the onset of a new one, might prevent you from completing your ITT. The most frequently mentioned health-related complaint that the student teachers we interviewed talked about was *stress*, and some ex-trainees attributed their experience of stress partly or wholly to their experience of ITT:

> [I find it] very, very, very stressful . . . I wish that I could relax but I can't. . . . I'm now suffering from breathlessness at night . . . I don't think any other job has so much pressure on them to prove themselves all the time . . . I developed asthma because of all this stress and that's what broke the camel's back.
>
> (Female, 40–44, primary)

> I felt myself having panic attacks. I found that I couldn't, I stopped planning lessons. I stopped writing anything down.
>
> (Male, 40–44, secondary)

Sometimes, depending in part on the specific cause(s) and the extent of the problem, *deferral* might be an option rather than complete withdrawal. Yet in a situation where you have made a serious attempt to identify and deal with the causes of stress and this has been unsuccessful, it may be that withdrawal is the best option for you. Just as people differ in how much pain they can bear, so it is with stress. If you have a low(-ish) stress threshold, it is possible that teaching (or learning teaching anyway) is in fact unhealthy and too stressful for *you*.

8 Lack of enjoyment of teaching and/or ITT

Prior to her decision to withdraw from her programme, one of the ex-trainees we talked to said that as a result of undertaking an ITT programme she had 'turned into a whinging teacher [and] a complete and utter bore'.

If you are not enjoying your ITT in general or the teaching aspect of ITT, or teaching in one placement school in particular, what would you put this down to? Can it be explained by any of the other issues that we have discussed above? If so, you could try working through the strategies we have suggested (here and elsewhere in the book) and seeing whether the situation improves and you start to enjoy teaching (and your ITT programme) more.

If you have given it your best and you still do not enjoy teaching, however, then (again) withdrawing from ITT might be the best option for you.

It is worth noting though that some of the factors associated with student teacher withdrawal, such as pupil discipline and other problems with school placements, are not necessarily issues that you will face in *all* schools. Remember that not all schools are the same. It is perfectly feasible that you could be very *unhappy* in your current school yet *happy* in your next one (if you continue to a next one).

To continue, to withdraw or to defer: making your decision

If, like the 11 per cent of (ex-)student teachers in our research, you don't feel there is *anything* that could prevent you from withdrawing from your ITT programme, and if you feel that you have done everything possible to address the problems you have faced but that this has not helped, then the decision not to complete your ITT might be for the best for you. Whether or not this is actually the best option for you will depend on the nature and seriousness of the problems you are facing, and the extent to which the strategies that you have put in place to try to deal with them might be helping already and might potentially help further in the future. Have you checked this out? Could it be that you are so 'down' that you are just not noticing the improvements, however slight?

Becoming a skilled teacher requires time, commitment, energy, diligence, tenacity, and resilience (both physical and emotional). And it is true that not everyone has the qualities, characteristics and current circumstances required to become a successful student and beginner teacher. Some individuals may have the qualities but circumstances militate against them. Others may have the potential but, for whatever reasons, do not have or are not willing or able to give adequate time to hone their skills. And a decision to withdraw from ITT is sometimes in your and others' best interests, for example if your teaching abilities (your ability to facilitate pupil learning) are showing little potential for improvement.

But do remember that if you are considering this step you will inevitably be feeling a bit gloomy, and may have forgotten that ToTs on your programme believed you had what it takes (or they would not have selected you). You may also, especially if you are somewhat of a perfectionist or you expected to be able to learn teaching quite quickly, need to check out with others what their perspective is on your progress and potential. Don't just assume you know – ask, and ask a number of people!

Perhaps especially where your reasons for considering withdrawal seem to centre around possibly temporary personal circumstances, deferral, or the possibility of returning to ITT at some time in the future, might be a better option for you. Indeed, not all of those who withdraw from ITT are necessarily lost to the profession for good. In our research 41 (30 per cent) of the 135 survey respondents who had withdrawn from ITT said they might return at some point in the future.

Finally, if you do decide that, whatever your circumstances or feelings may be in the future, returning to ITT is not a desirable option, and you therefore choose to withdraw from ITT, do try to remember that there will still be much that you have gained and learned from your experience which might be helpful to you in the future, e.g. in your next chosen career. If you are one of these people, what do you think you might have learned? You may, for example, have a better idea of:

- your strengths and limitations;
- whether you enjoy working with children and/or adults;
- whether you enjoy working under pressure;
- what transferable skills you have developed;
- the types of jobs and circumstances you do and do not enjoy working in.

Conclusion

If you turned first to this chapter in the book, perhaps because you were already in crisis, we hope you have found some positive ways forward, whether you stay in, defer completion of, or leave your ITT programme. If you are currently following an ITT programme but have yet to sink into a pit of despair, take heart; you may never do so. Only a very small minority of people in our research found themselves in this position – but do use the ideas in the book and chapter to help ensure that you never do! Remember the mantras 'if you always do what you've always done, you'll always get what you've always got' and 'talk to people' and 'do something' about any problems as and when they arise. If, on the other hand, you are reading this before you start your ITT programme, or when trying to make up your mind whether or not to undertake ITT, we hope this will have helped to paint a picture of what it *can* be (and has been) like for a few people, and so help you make an even more informed decision.

In the next and final chapter we discuss – for those readers who have had a more positive experience of ITT and still want to become teachers – means of finding and securing your first teaching post.

Section 3

Moving beyond initial teacher training and looking ahead

Chapter 9

'I just got this feeling when I walked in; I felt that I would fit there'

Finding and securing your first teaching post

Introduction

In many parts of the world, newly qualified teachers are *allocated* posts. That is, they are told which school they are to work in and have no choice. If you are in such a position, you are perhaps fortunate in that you know you will have work and you have fewer decisions to make. And this chapter is not for you! If, on the other hand, you are in a similar position to those student teachers in our research study and need to search out, apply and compete for vacant posts, the insights from our research participants' experiences may help you in making this next set of important decisions and preparations, which can lead to you being able to find and secure the best job for you.

In this chapter we discuss a range of issues associated with applying for teaching posts. Drawing on our research findings and our own experience both of gaining teaching posts and of appointing people to them, we offer a number of suggestions both to help you decide what type of post to look for and to help you secure your first post as a newly qualified teacher. We begin by pointing out that the process of applying for and attempting to secure a teaching post can be a demanding and even potentially a stressful one – especially, perhaps, if you leave it too late to start thinking about it!

Pressures associated with looking for a teaching post

Looking for, applying for and attempting to secure an appropriate teaching post can be a particularly testing process when (as most trainees do) you undertake this process alongside the usual pressures of following an ITT programme. First, there are the pressures associated with finding or making the time to apply for posts and to attend job interviews. Amidst the demands of teaching placements, course assignments and a life outside ITT, it is easy to put off the task of looking for a job, as suggested by the following quotation from one of the student teachers we spoke to:

> I didn't have the time or the energy, I just wanted to focus on a good [teaching] practice instead of spending time filling in forms, and again I didn't have that much time between . . . doing my coursework, looking after my family, all the rest of it.
>
> (Female, 25–29, primary)

An obvious danger of 'putting it off', however, is that you may miss the opportunity to apply for some of the best available jobs – and perhaps the one that is most right for you.

Another pressure that some trainees find difficult and you might mentally prepare yourself for is the possibility that you may be in 'competition' for teaching posts with your fellow trainees:

> It was all a bit strange to be honest because . . . there were three of us going for the same post and it was all suddenly a bit cloak and dagger and these people are my friends.
>
> (Male, 30–34, primary)

Third, for those of you who don't manage to secure a post via your first couple of applications, there is a potential for self-doubt and insecurity to creep in, and the possibility that you might begin to become 'desperate', which can lead you to a situation in which you might end up accepting the 'wrong' job:

> [I]t is not about the actual teaching job it is more about the kind of atmosphere I will be working in, it is more about the type of school, if the school is a caring type of school or whatever, and the staff and all that . . . because I was getting desperate as well and I was just thinking 'I have no job, I have got to take it, I have got to take it'.
>
> (Female, 30–34, primary)

There is a tension, then, between: (1) the need (in most cases) to get *a* job, and perhaps to get a job as soon as possible, in order to earn much-needed money, to pay the bills and/or support a family; and (2) the desire to obtain a post *which suits you*. To help you address this issue, it will be helpful for you to consider, and in some cases find the answers to, some important questions, including:

- How much do I need a job?
- How soon do I need to secure a teaching post or how long could I manage without one?
- What sort of teaching post would I like?
- Would I be happy to work as a supply teacher if necessary until I manage to find a job that is right for me?

- How mobile am I? (Can I relocate?)
- How many relevant jobs are coming up or likely to come up in that part (or those parts) of the country/world I would like to work in?

You might try jotting down your immediate answers to these questions. The ones that are hardest for you to answer may be the ones you need to discuss with your family or friends, or on which you might seek advice from your tutors, or for which you need to do more research. But do think about coming back to these same questions at the end of the chapter. We hope that by that time your answers to at least some of the questions will be more comprehensive.

What should you look for in a teaching post?

At this point it would be helpful to you to refer back to your checklist about what it is that you like(d) and dislike(d) about the particular schools that you visited before or during your ITT. We suggested that you develop such a checklist in Chapter 4. If you did, it might be helpful at this stage to review what you wrote and see whether you would like to add anything to the list. If you didn't, we suggest that you think back to the time you have spent in different schools and develop your checklist now! Having (and periodically updating) such a checklist will be helpful to you:

1 in deciding which jobs to apply to (based on the information about the school that is provided and that you can discover);
2 in reminding you what to look out for when you are visiting a school or attending an interview; and (thus)
3 in helping you to work out whether you are likely to enjoy working there and whether or not to accept the job if it is offered to you.

Let us now see if the student teachers in our research had similar ideas to you, and if some of their ideas might give you some new ideas and enable you to develop your checklist further.

The student teachers in our survey were asked, at the end of their ITT courses, what attracted them to particular teaching posts. Their answers are summarised in Table 9.1. The most frequently mentioned considerations were:

- the 'convenient geographical location' of the school (29 per cent);
- the school had 'a good track record' (22 per cent); and
- perceived 'staff collegiality/teamwork' (21 per cent).

Some of the other responses to the survey, and some of the things the trainees we spoke to told us about what attracted them to a teaching post,

Table 9.1 What would you say are the things which attracted you to the post?

	No.	%
Convenient geographic location	554	29
School with a good track record	426	22
Staff collegiality/teamwork	398	21
It was an ITT placement school	244	13
Wanted to live close to where my family lives	197	10
Good environment/atmosphere/school	145	8
Wanted to work in the area where I lived while I was a trainee	138	7
First job offer	105	6
Staff are friendly/pleasant	96	5
The subject/course/curriculum	94	5
The age of pupils/students	92	5
Opportunities for career progression	81	4
School with experience of working with NQTs	77	4
Challenging pupils	75	4
Attractive salary	72	4
Opportunities for professional learning	57	3
Denominational or faith school	56	3
School in challenging circumstances	54	3
Good facilities	51	3
Small school	50	3
No. of cases	1,919	

More than one response could be given so percentages do not sum to 100.

were also related to these three points. For example, with respect to obtaining a post in a 'convenient geographical location', 10 per cent of survey respondents said they were attracted to a particular post because they wanted to live close to their families, another 7 per cent said they wanted to work in the area where they lived as a trainee, and some of the trainees we spoke to said that family and child care considerations affected the distance they would be able to travel in order to take up a teaching post:

> I drew a circle round where I lived because I have child care issues and I needed to be able to get there and back, and I saw this school.
>
> (Female, 30–34, secondary)

With regard to the attraction of obtaining a post in a school or department that appeared to be characterised by collegiality and teamwork, another 8 per cent of survey respondents described the schools they were attracted to as having a 'good environment' or 'atmosphere', while 5 per cent said they were attracted by their perception that the staff were 'friendly' or 'pleasant', and these considerations were reflected in comments made by the trainees we spoke to, some of whom emphasised the importance of 'the school ethos' and of being able to 'get on' with the people they would be working with:

> Lovely bunch of people in the IT department and I thought 'if I get offered the job I'll take it' because I just got this feeling when I walked in, I felt that I would fit there.
>
> (Female, 30–34, secondary)

> They seem to have a really positive team spirit . . . As soon as I walked in I felt I really liked the environment, it was really nice, it's really productive and I think that's given me a lot of support.
>
> (Female, 30–34, primary)

However, in relation to the school having a 'good track record', whereas some of the beginner teachers we spoke to were attracted by the idea of teaching pupils who 'wanted to learn', others were attracted to working with more challenging pupils (such as the 4 per cent of survey respondents in Table 9.1) or in more challenging schools (such as the 3 per cent of survey respondents):

> As an NQT I think it will help me that the kids are so high achievers, that takes away a big boundary, you know. It is like, from what I can gather, if you lead them to water they will drink, which is brilliant, that makes my life easier.
>
> (Male, 25–29, secondary)

> He said, you know, it is a challenging school . . . There is a lot of work going on with the kids and [child] protection, stuff like that, so that to me sounded very interesting as well, you know.
>
> (Female, 45 or over, secondary)

Which kind of pupils would *you* prefer to teach – ones who 'want to learn', those who are more of a 'challenge', or both (or those who are a combination of the two)?

Some of the NQTs we interviewed had actually obtained posts in challenging schools, and some described what they saw as the positive aspects of working in such schools, as the following illustrates:

> I like working here because it's a challenge, well it could be a challenge if we didn't have the behavioural policies that we have which is fantastic, it's very, very firm and very, very fair. The area is very, very deprived . . . When you tell people you work in [place] they're like 'what? What are you doing there?!' But it's fabulous because they really work hard and yes they've got problems but you can understand why they have problems. Whereas sometimes on placement when I was having real problems it was just that they [the pupils] were spoilt. You think, 'what's your problem? I don't understand.' At least here, if something happens you can see why. The kids are really nice.
>
> (Female, 20–24, primary)

On the other hand, some NQTs warn others not to follow in their footsteps:

> Basically it's been an experience but I would never, never in a million years recommend anybody to come to a Special Measures school,[1] [it's] too much for an NQT. Even though [what] I've learnt in a year compared to other [NQTs] is immense, which will hopefully be a reward later in life, it's a make or break thing. Sometimes it could break you and you would never want to go into teaching or . . . [you'd] think 'I don't want to work in schools like this', and you get really disheartened.
>
> (Female, 20–24, primary)

One of the potential problems of working in very challenging schools is that some (sometimes many) of the established teachers are so focused on dealing with difficult pupils or improving their own performance that they may have less time and energy to commit to supporting the specific needs of an NQT. Again, however, *different* kinds of pressures may be associated with getting a job in a high-achieving school, including issues relating to parental expectations:

> The expectations are so much higher. I mean, this is the sort of school where parents come and say 'What will you be doing with my child today?' You know, 'I want to know what you will be teaching them.'
>
> (Female, 35–39, primary)

Other considerations that emerged from both our survey and our research interviews were the importance, to some trainees, of trying to secure posts in schools that would:

- provide support for their individual needs as NQTs;
- provide support for their professional learning; and

- provide opportunities for career progression.

You may remember that in Chapter 3 we reported some responses, given by the beginning teachers in our research, to the question 'If you could give one piece of advice to someone considering becoming a teacher, what would it be?' Some of the responses we didn't tell you about then relate to issues that these NQTs seemed to feel they had not paid enough attention to when they had looked for their first post and, with hindsight, wished they had. They reflect – and develop further – some of the points we have made above:

> Make sure that the department you are going into is well run and that there is good cohesion!
>
> (Male, 20–24, secondary)

> Ensure that you have support from the Senior Leadership re. behaviour and the like and ensure that the school has implemented support for the Workload Agreement[2] such as admin[istrative] assistance and photocopying. As an NQT you need support for a range of issues.
>
> (Male, 20–24, secondary)

> Never start [your teaching career] in a Special Measures school!!! Always find out how the NQTs are supported.
>
> (Female, 20–24, primary).

When we spoke to NQTs at the end of their first year of teaching, and to those who completed their second year of teaching, we found that the availability (or lack) of support remained a key factor in whether or not they had enjoyed teaching and, for some, whether or not they intended to remain in teaching.

Working in an ITT placement school

We saw in Table 9.1 that 13 per cent of the respondents to our end-of-ITT-course survey said they were attracted to particular teaching posts by the fact that they were based at one of their ITT placement schools. And around a third (32 per cent) of the newly qualified teachers in our research actually obtained posts in schools where they had done at least some of their ITT. Although this percentage was boosted by and was inevitably much higher amongst those who had followed employment-based ITT routes (e.g. 58 per cent of respondents from the GRTP route were working in one of their ITT schools one year after completing their ITT), as many as 26 per cent of respondents from the university-administered PGCE route also managed to get a job in an ITT placement school. We might add that those NQTs who had reported positive relationships with mentors and other teaching staff in their ITT placement schools were more likely to have acquired a job in one of these schools, which again emphasises the importance of establishing good, meaningful working relations with colleagues in your placement schools.

One of the things that attracted some beginner teachers to jobs in one of their ITT placement schools was that they felt already integrated into the school, so the transition to becoming a newly qualified teacher was perhaps less daunting:

> I really wanted to stay at the school where I am . . . I suppose you get used to one particular way of doing things . . . I suppose I've always liked the way the school where I am does things . . . Then going out and seeing other schools, it was quite an eye opener and I think I'm never going to find anywhere [else] where I'm going to feel at home.
>
> (Female, 40–44, primary)

> [T]o go to a different school would've been a lot more stressful because you've got to learn the way they work, the people, the students, lots of different things. A number of the schemes I've taught this year I had started to teach last year.
>
> (Female 40–44, secondary)

So, if you felt 'at home' there and if it is an option for you, getting a job in an ITT placement school, and thus ensuring some continuity and stability, can be a sensible move in a context in which there will be plenty of other changes in the move from student teacher to NQT to keep you busy! Yet there are potential pros *and* cons of obtaining a post in one of your placement schools and doing so will be more 'right' for some readers than for others. For example, one downside is that, having worked with you as a trainee, some of your new colleagues may not regard you as an established teacher and may continue to treat you as a 'student'. On the other hand, doing so may remind your colleagues that as an NQT you are still a relative novice, and may encourage them to provide more support than might be the case should you secure a post in a 'new' school.

How easy (or hard) will it be to find a job?

The answer to this question will depend on a number of factors, including:

- supply and demand (the availability of teaching posts and the numbers of people applying for the posts available);
- (within that) whether or not your subject specialism, especially if you have trained to teach at secondary level, is in short supply;
- whether or not you manage to find out about all – or the majority of – posts that are actually available;
- how many posts you can manage to find the time to apply to ('You've gotta be in it to win it!');
- how willing or able you are to relocate (how geographically mobile you are);
- how long your list of essential characteristics (criteria) is regarding the type of post that you are willing to apply for and accept;
- how well you sell yourself and 'perform' at interview; and
- how far and how well you heed the advice of your course tutors and the advice we provide below, in which we address many of the issues listed above!

What difficulties might I encounter in finding a job?

One year after they completed their ITT, we asked 2,406 newly qualified teachers whether they had encountered any difficulties when looking for a teaching post. Just under a quarter of those questioned (23 per cent) said they had experienced difficulties in this regard (77 per cent said they hadn't). The 545 NQTs who reported experiencing difficulties in finding a job were then asked what these difficulties were. The main reasons given included:

- 'couldn't find a post in the location I wanted' (34 per cent);
- 'couldn't find any type of post' (15 per cent);
- 'couldn't find a permanent post' (10 per cent);
- 'too many people applying for the same job' (9 per cent);
- 'lacked sufficient experience for the posts available' (6 per cent).

The biggest single obstacle to finding a job, then, was location – or geographical mobility. Some of the NQTs we interviewed experienced and talked about this problem, as illustrated in the following quotation:

> [T]here were absolutely no jobs, unless I was prepared to move way out of the area, there were plenty of jobs if I went further up north. I actually had, I met somebody on holiday, a head teacher, and they were offering me a position, or to come up and be interviewed for a position . . . because they were crying out for teachers, they couldn't get teachers up there. That, I found very disillusioning.
>
> (Female, 30–34, primary)

The second most popular answer – 'couldn't find any type of post' – is slightly more unusual and suggests that either the NQTs weren't looking in the right places for job advertisements (see below), or they had already narrowed their search in some way.

With regard to the third point – 'couldn't find a permanent post' – this suggests a particular criterion on the checklists of some applicants for their first post, that is, relative job security, which wasn't always available. How important is this to you?

We have encouraged you to identify the characteristics of schools that you would most like to work in, and of the type of post you would like to obtain; however, at this point, having seen that some beginner teachers find it difficult to secure posts, or to secure the kind of post they would like, it might be sensible for you to put your criteria (desirable characteristics) into an order of priority in case it becomes doubtful that you will be able to get *everything* that you would ideally look for in a teaching post and you need to compromise somewhere. You could, for example, group your characteristics into 'essential' (must have) and 'desirable' (would also like to have, if possible). In other words, you may need to trade off one criterion or ideal characteristic against another. In particular, those of you who are less willing or able to relocate geographically may have to be 'less fussy' regarding other desirable criteria!

Finally in this section, we saw that 6 per cent of those survey respondents who had difficulties in finding a job said that one of the reasons for this was that they lacked sufficient experience for the posts available, and some of the NQTs we spoke to made the same point:

> [T]hey wanted someone with more experience, rather than an NQT. And one interview that I went to . . . at the end of it the feedback was, 'oh we didn't really want an NQT' . . . And a lot of them were like, 'well you need more experience before we can give you a job'.
> (Female, 22–26, primary)

Although this problem may reflect a genuine lack of suitable teaching posts in relation to specific subject specialisms, it might also suggest that, in some cases, the beginner teachers may have applied for posts that were not really appropriate for NQTs. Clues about this are often provided in the job advertisements or the 'further particulars' – but not always, and sometimes an interview panel's preference for a more experienced candidate only emerges on the day! Nevertheless, if a job advertisement or the further particulars you have sent off for include phrases such as 'experienced teacher required' then it is usually wise to save your energies for applying for more suitable posts. Some advertisements and further particulars are extremely helpful, on the other hand, and use phrases such as 'NQTs are welcome to apply'. This sometimes suggests that the school has a limited budget for the appointment and you could therefore be at an *advantage* over a more experienced (and more expensive) teacher!

Where do I find out about available teaching posts?

The answer to this question will obviously vary to some extent across different countries and in different states/regions of the same country, but the trainees in our research said they had found out about job vacancies in the following places:

- advertisements in national newspapers (for example, in England, the *Times Educational Supplement*);
- advertisements in local newspapers;
- the internet;
- their ITT courses/tutors;
- notice boards (e.g. in your ITT placement schools);
- personal recommendations.

If you need or want to get work immediately on completion of your ITT programme, we suggest you put aside some time every week from at least six months before the end of your programme to research vacancies. Perhaps you can make it a 'big rock', or at least a sizeable 'pebble'! (See Chapter 4.)

Once you have found out about vacant posts, you can begin to compare the information provided about them against your checklist. Then you need to write off, to those which seem to offer all or most of the 'essential' criteria, for the 'further particulars', and check again. It will make this process quicker if you devise a 'writing for further particulars' template letter once, and store it electronically to reuse (amending as appropriate) each time.

Prepare yourself for the application and appointment process

This process of applying and being considered for a teaching post can involve a range of activities, including:

- submitting a formal application, which might include one or more of a letter of application, a CV and a completed application form;
- being shown around the school;
- having informal discussions;
- being formally interviewed by a panel of interviewers;
- being asked to teach a lesson;
- being asked to plan a lesson or a scheme of work;
- meeting (and/or being interviewed by) pupils.

We say 'can involve' because what is actually required in this regard is likely to vary from school to school. Whatever is involved, however, it will be important that you (a) find this out; and (b) prepare yourself well for each element (see 'tips' below). And whatever the process, each element, whether informal (a chat, a tour, encounters with pupils) or more formal (an interview, a completed form, a letter) will have been included to provide an opportunity not only for 'them' to see if you are what they are looking for, but also for you to see if the school and post suit *you*. If there is a formal interview, this will often end the process, and will frequently include a question about whether or not, given all your experiences in and of the school, you are still interested in the post. As it will help you (and them) if you can justify your answer, it may help to bear your checklist in mind as you go through the process.

Questions to find answers to when you visit a school

When you visit or are in a school as part of a job application process, you will inevitably be noticing all sorts of things: about the people in it and how they interact with each other and with you, about the buildings, decor and facilities, about any evidence that gives you a clue about what seems to be important to and in the school, and so on. This will be important in helping you get a sense of what the school and job might be like and whether or not it would suit you. But it would help you notice more, and notice more usefully for you, if you looked carefully at your checklist beforehand and considered what kinds of things, if you noticed them, would suggest the school or job was 'for you', or alternatively what might be a 'deal-breaker'. You could then devise a set of questions to bear in mind to guide your observations or what kinds of things you might ask, which can help you build a picture of the school and how it works, and help you to decide whether it is 'right' for you.

These questions might include, for example:

- Which teachers and support staff will you be working with? What do you notice about how they seem to work? What evidence do you have of this? Where are their desks or work-stations? (Do they have any?) Where would yours be in relation to theirs?
- What do the head teacher and head of department seem like to you? Where are their offices? Are they alone or with others there? Are the doors open or closed? Do you notice them interacting with other teachers? How?
- If a mentor role exists in your system for newly qualified teachers, who will be your mentor? What do they seem like to you? Do they volunteer something about themselves? Have they been a mentor

before? Do they ask you about you? Do they seem to be committed to the role and to helping/supporting you?

- What are the pupils like? How do they interact with each other, with the teachers, with you?

> I basically walked through the school and got lost a lot, every time I got lost I grabbed a student and asked 'can you show me?' I wanted to see the students without a head teacher next to me, and I didn't meet a student who wasn't polite and they seemed very enthusiastic, yes they had different life experience, very much city kids . . . But they seemed really bouncy and bubbly.
>
> (Female, 30–34, secondary)

- What are the buildings and facilities like? What is displayed on the walls? Who seems to be the intended audience for the displays? (Visitors? Parents? Pupils?)

You will also need to find out what support will be in place for you, and determine if, for example, the school is aware of, and provisions are in place to ensure that you will receive, any entitlements to which you are due as a newly qualified teacher. (For example, in England NQTs are entitled to 10 per cent of non-contact time during the school week, over and above that due to other teachers.) If there are any and you get the opportunity, you could talk to other teachers who have recently completed their first year in teaching to find out how it went for them and whether they received their entitlements, if these exist in your system, and whether they felt they had sufficient support and access to relevant training courses.

Additional tips to help you secure a post

The following are some additional tips to help you to both find the best job for you and be successful in getting it. They are drawn from our own and our research participants' experience.

- Always acquire and study the further information provided about a post (and the school in which it is based) *before* applying for the post.
- Follow the instructions carefully in developing your application. For example, if the head teacher asks for a letter of application, make sure it looks like a *letter*.
- You will normally be required to give the names, addresses and contact details of two or more referees. Out of courtesy (and to give you an indication of whether they would be able to give you a good reference) always ask those who you are thinking of naming as referees whether they are willing and able to support your application.

- Always tailor your application to the specific post you are applying for. Research what your potential employers are likely to be looking for and make sure that your application explicitly addresses the job criteria in the further particulars.
- Write a draft application first and ask a tutor or mentor to look at it, before revising it in light of the comments they give you.
- Always proof read your 'completed' application (and ask someone else to do so) before you submit it. Spelling mistakes and typos will give the impression of carelessness and raise questions about your attention to detail.
- Make sure you include any details that are requested. For example, if an application form asks for the postal and email addresses and telephone numbers of your previous employers and your referees, be sure to provide *all* of this. If you don't know some of the information to start with (as is often the case), *then find it out*. If you omit some information it could look as if you are disorganised, lazy or careless, or perhaps all three!
- Find out about the school you are applying to and demonstrate knowledge of the school both in your application and during the interview day, if you are invited for interview.
- Prepare *thoroughly* for any tasks you are asked to undertake on the day.
- Research the kinds of questions you are likely to be asked at interview and think about how you would answer them, but try to avoid giving any 'scripted' answers on the day.
- During the interview make sure you listen to the questions carefully and take a few seconds to think about your answer to each question before you start talking. Address your answer primarily to the person who asked the question, though ensure you make eye-contact with all members of the interview panel.
- If possible, take part in a mock interview. If your ITT programme doesn't provide the opportunity for you to do this, perhaps you could organise it yourself with fellow trainees or at your placement school.
- If you are given the opportunity to visit/look around a school before applying for the post or before attending for an interview, do make every effort to take this up. This might enable you to demonstrate an interest in the school and to get a 'feel' for the school, and (if it occurs at an early stage) might enhance your ability to tailor the application form and/or your interview preparation to the specific demands of the post. If you are provided with the opportunity to visit but don't take it up, it may be interpreted as a lack of interest in the job or school. But if the possibility to visit the school ahead of the interview day isn't mentioned in any of the literature, they might think you are 'too demanding' or 'too pushy' if you try to arrange this.

> I took it [the application form] in and had a look around the school, and I think that helped me an awful lot . . . Not only do you get a feel for the school, the head or whoever is showing you round gets to get a feel for you, it has just got to be a help.
>
> (Male, 20–24, primary)

- Make sure you have prepared some questions to ask at an appropriate moment (e.g. at the end of the formal interview). But *adapt* your 'pre-prepared' questions as appropriate so (for example) you ask only ones for which the 'answer' hasn't already been provided during the interview or the day.
- Put modesty to one side. Try to ensure you have discussed, written about or otherwise made visible *all* your strengths so that the types of positive contributions you could/would make in the post are clear. In other words, sell yourself. And sell your ITT course too – for example, by pointing to the valuable ways in which it has prepared you to be an effective teacher.
- Find out what support and professional development opportunities are available to you as an NQT. You need to know that you will receive your entitlements, and you want them to think that you are willing and keen to learn and develop as a teacher, but you don't want to give the impression that you will require *too much* help!
- Show that you can be serious but also that you have a sense of humour. Those on the appointment panel want to know whether they will be able to (and would like to) work (and spend time) with you. But be yourself.
- Always ask for feedback on your application and interview technique. If you don't get the job, the advice you gain might help you to get the next one.

> [T]hey said I didn't sell myself, I wasn't positive enough. I have to say that was just before Easter, I was feeling very low at that point, so I think he was probably very correct. I didn't feel very positive about myself. I was determined on the next ones that I would be very cheerful and sell myself, which obviously worked.
>
> (Female, 45 or over, secondary)

Working as a supply teacher

Finally, if it is taking time to find the right post for you, or to persuade an appointment panel to give you a job that *you* feel is right for you, one option, rather than take 'any' job, or the 'wrong job', or a job that doesn't meet all of your 'essential' criteria, may be to undertake paid 'supply' or 'cover' teaching, filling in for temporarily absent teachers. In fact, when we surveyed the teachers in our research project one year after they completed their ITT, as many as 26 per cent said they had worked as supply teachers during the previous year. Supply teaching has a number of advantages and disadvantages compared with 'standard' (permanent or fixed-term) teaching posts. On the downside, for example:

- There is the uncertainty about whether you will be offered enough supply work on a week-to-week or day-to-day basis.
- You don't normally enjoy the same benefits of holiday pay and pension contributions.
- Unless you manage to secure a relatively long-term 'cover' position, supply teaching can be quite a lonely experience in which you may not feel that you have a 'home' and may find it difficult to establish meaningful relationships with pupils or colleagues.

On the upside, however:

- The workload tends to be lighter because there is less preparation and marking, and fewer meetings to attend!
- It may be more interesting to experience a wider range of teaching and learning environments, which
  - might help your professional development;
  - might give you further ideas about the kinds of school (or which specific schools) you would like to work in; and
  - might enable you to make a good impression in schools that could be looking for new teachers in the future!

Some of these points are illustrated in the following quotations from two of our interviewees who were working as supply teachers:

> I am with one or two agencies . . . there doesn't seem to be tons of work . . . I think it is a case of getting your toe in the door and once you have done that you are OK. This is what I have been told, just plodding on and something will turn up.
>
> (Female, 30–34, primary)

> I mean obviously I would prefer to have a job for September because it would be nice to have my own class, but if not I am quite happy just to get more different experiences in different schools, with different children.
>
> (Female, 20–24, primary)

Conclusion

In this chapter we have suggested that, even though you may feel that you have quite enough to do getting through your ITT course, if you want to secure the best post for you on completing your ITT, then you will need to put in effort to do so, and approach the task with informed determination. We have shared the tips and hints that our own experience, as well as that of our research participants, has suggested can help in this process of finding and applying for jobs. Finally, try not to get disheartened if you don't get the first 'perfect job' you apply for. As with anything, as long as you work at learning the lessons from each attempt, you *will* get better – and anyway, the job can't have been as perfect for you as it seemed at first or 'they' *would* have hired you!

We turn now to our final thoughts in this book, which we hope will be (or has been or is being) a useful companion in helping you to navigate the demanding early stages of the process of becoming a teacher. In our concluding chapter we give some brief insights into what you might look forward to about being a newly qualified teacher.

Conclusion

'Ditching the student teacher tag'

In this book we have addressed the main issues relating to initial teacher training that student teachers are concerned about and which impact on their experience. In doing so, we suggested a number of ways of thinking, and strategies, which were designed to enable you to make more informed and appropriate decisions and (for those of you who did become student teachers) help you feel more in control of the roller-coaster ride that undertaking an ITT course can be.

If you have read this book in order to help you make up your mind about whether or not to undertake an ITT course, we trust it will have given you a better idea of what it might be like, how you would or could cope, and whether or not teaching might suit you (or you it). If you have decided to go for it and apply for or start a course, 'forewarned is forearmed' and you already have a useful resource to turn to in times of need. If, however, you have decided that teaching is not for you, we hope the book has not only helped you to make the right decision for you but has also given you a better insight into one of the most important professions in any society.

Perhaps you are already a student teacher and you initially picked up or were recommended this book because of one or two particular chapters. If so, we hope you also had the chance to look at all of them, if only in order to know they are there, and where you might look should (though we are tempted to write 'when'!) any of the other issues become relevant for you.

If this book has been a useful companion to you during your ITT, perhaps it may remain so as (if) you continue on your journey through the early stages in the process of becoming a teacher. In other words, it is likely that many of the issues we have discussed here will remain relevant to you over the next few years at least, particularly perhaps each time you take on a new responsibility and challenge. We say this because, when we interviewed the NQTs who took part in our research at the end of their first year in post, we discovered that most encountered both 'high' and 'low' points throughout the school year (and sometimes even during the same working day!), and the causes of these 'highs' and 'lows' were mostly familiar. As was the case during ITT, the 'lows' experienced by NQTs most often related to (1) workload and work–life balance; and (2) challenging relationships with pupils, with pupils' parents and/or with colleagues in their schools.

But there were lots of 'highs' too, and these were associated mostly with:

- the development of positive relationships with pupils;
- NQTs' perceptions of pupil learning and development, and their role in fostering this;
- the development of positive relationships with teacher colleagues;
- the feeling of being part of a team;
- an increased sense of autonomy, including having 'their own' classroom and 'their own' pupils, establishing 'their own' classroom routines and being able to be more flexible in their lesson planning and teaching than had been possible during their ITT;
- being recognised as, trusted as and treated like a ('real') teacher.

So if you are about to embark on your first year as a qualified teacher, there are more challenges ahead, and some familiar ones, and we hope the suggestions we have made in this book will help you to (continue to) deal with them. There is also a lot to look forward to. In fact, when we asked those who were just completing their ITT courses what they were most looking forward to about their first year as a qualified teacher, the most common responses were:

- 'having my own class';
- 'having my own class *for a whole year*'; and
- 'being a "proper" teacher'.

The following quotations illustrate these ideas.

> [What I am] most looking forward to would be just having my own classes and my own responsibilities with those. Starting with the pupils from day one and being able to set my own standards and my own rules rather than following somebody else's. So that I'm really looking forward to.
>
> (Female, 40–44, secondary)

> What I really want to see [is] that having started the class from September [I will] see them growing [over] one year. I think that has become very important for me.
>
> (Female, 25–29, primary)

> I think it would be nice to ditch that student teacher tag . . . it would be nice I think to be going in there and [feel like] you are actually a full teacher, a fully qualified teacher and you are, you know, you have a right to be there.
>
> (Female, 25–29, secondary)

[B]eing able to just like be a real teacher if you know what I mean. The realistic side of it that you know you can change things and be flexible and that sort of thing.

(Female, 20–24, primary)

The fact that many (completing) student teachers eagerly anticipated having 'their own' class, and were looking forward to the increase in autonomy and the added responsibility that this would bring, is a positive reflection on their ITT programmes. So, those of you reading this before undertaking an ITT programme or in the early stages of your programme can feel reassured by the knowledge that the programmes followed by these student teachers had supported them in their development to the stage that they were, and felt themselves to be, ready for such responsibilities.

It may also be reassuring to know, as (or if) you are approaching your first year as a qualified teacher, that the vast majority (93 per cent) of NQTs in our research reported (at the end of their first year) that they enjoyed working as teachers. In addition, the majority of NQTs also reported 'good' or 'very good' relationships with teaching colleagues (97 per cent), pupils (97 per cent), non-teaching staff (96 per cent), pupils' parents (89 per cent) and head teachers (82 per cent). Only 4 per cent of survey respondents indicated that they had not enjoyed working as teachers. We should add that those NQTs who gave more positive ratings of their *relationships with other teachers* were more likely to enjoy working as teachers. So, for one last time, it really is worth doing your very best to build and maintain healthy working relationships!

Another point that we'd like to make for one last time is that we hope you will never stop regarding yourself as a learner – there is *always* more to learn, even for experienced teachers. Related to this, and the final point we would like to make 'for the last time', is to remember that not everything goes well all of the time – for *anyone*! So (again) try not to worry too much when some things inevitably do go wrong. Rather, consider what you can learn from the experience, 'move on', and remind yourself what is going 'right'.

We said in the Introduction to this book that we saw the process of writing and reading as engaging in a kind of 'dialogue at a distance'. If you would like to engage in more direct dialogue, we would be very interested in hearing from you about whether (and if so when, how, and in what ways) you have found this book useful, or about any other comments on the book you would like to make, including how we might improve it for future readers (and potential teachers of tomorrow). Our email addresses can be found below.

- hbsnndy@googlemail.com
- amalderez@googlemail.com
- louisectracey@googlemail.com

Finally, whether you are engaged in the process of becoming and developing as a teacher or you have decided that teaching is not for you and that you will follow a different career path, we wish you a long and rewarding career.

Appendix
How we learned about student teachers' experiences

Introduction

As teachers of teachers we advise our students that, when reading about research, they should always consider:

- the sources of evidence (if any) that people use to back up what they say;
- how that evidence was arrived at and dealt with and by whom; and
- when and where the research was undertaken.

This sort of information should then help them (and you) to decide how far they (you) trust the findings the authors have reported and how relevant they (you) judge it to be to their (your) circumstances. In this Appendix we provide you with a little more information than we have done hitherto about how we found out about the experiences of the student teachers we refer to throughout the book. We have already told you a little bit about ourselves in the Introduction.

The research upon which this book is based is known as the 'Becoming a Teacher' (BaT) project. The research was carried out between 2003 and 2009, and involved tracking a cohort of beginner teachers in England between their initial teacher training (ITT) and the end of their fourth year in post or, for some, the point at which they withdrew from their ITT or left teaching.

Who were the beginner teachers involved in our research?

To try to ensure that we ended up with a fairly representative group of beginner teachers in our research, we began by randomly selecting ITT providers, across England, for each of the main ITT routes. The main routes included:

- university-administered Postgraduate Certificate of Education (PGCE) programmes;

- Flexible PGCE programmes;
- Bachelor of Education (BEd) programmes;
- Bachelor of Arts (BA) and Bachelor of Science (BSc) with Qualified Teacher Status (QTS) programmes;
- School-Centred Initial Teacher Training (SCITT) programmes; and
- Graduate and Registered Teacher Programmes (GRTP).

(A brief outline of these different routes is provided in the introduction to Chapter 2.)

We then asked the course leaders of the 110 selected ITT providers if they would allow us access to the student teachers following (or about to begin) specific ITT programmes in their institutions, in order that we could invite them to participate in our research. Seventy-four providers agreed.

Annual surveys of beginner teachers

We next arranged to invite all student teachers on the specified programmes to complete a questionnaire survey. The questionnaire was completed by 4,790 student teachers, across England, who were beginning one-year ITT programmes or beginning their final year of two-, three- or four-year programmes. The questionnaire asked about a range of issues, including:

- the reasons they chose to undertake ITT;
- the reasons they chose the specific ITT route they were following;
- their concerns about ITT and teaching;
- what they were looking forward to about ITT and teaching;
- what elements of their programmes they felt would be most useful in helping them to learn about teaching and become a teacher.

A comparison between our questionnaire survey sample and the national profile of student teachers suggested that our survey participants were representative of all trainees by gender and ethnicity, across the range of ITT routes studied.[1]

The same beginner teachers were subsequently asked to take part in follow-up annual surveys. Of these, whose experiences are illustrated and discussed in this book:

- 3,162 took part in an end-of-ITT survey, which asked respondents about their experiences of undertaking ITT, including (for example) their relationships with their mentors and other teachers, whether they enjoyed ITT, and how well they felt their course had prepared them to become a teacher; and
- 2,446 took part in a survey, administered one year after they completed their ITT, which asked them about their experiences of their first year in post.

Interviews and ejournals

From those who took part in the original questionnaire survey, we selected 85 participants from different age groups, including men and women, those following different ITT routes, and those training to teach in both primary and secondary schools, to take part in additional research work which would enable us to explore beginner teachers' views and experiences in more detail than was possible in the survey. The numbers of beginner teachers involved this aspect of the research and on whose experiences we draw in this book are as follows:

- 85 took part in an initial interview about their reasons for undertaking ITT, their concerns and expectations about ITT and teaching, etc.; of whom
- 79 were re-interviewed at the end of their ITT programmes, about their experiences of ITT;
- 73 were interviewed one year after completing their ITT, about their experiences of their first year of teaching; and
- 46 took part in half-termly email exchanges ('ejournals'), throughout their first year in post, in which they told us about (for example) the highs, lows and other significant moments associated with their work and lives as newly qualified teachers.

Where can I find out more?

Further information about the 'Becoming a Teacher' research can be found on the project website at www.becoming-a-teacher.ac.uk.

More information about the methods of data generation, sampling and analysis that we employed, and more detailed accounts of the findings from the first few years of the 'Becoming a Teacher' research, can be found in the following publications:

Hobson, A. J., Tracey, L., Kerr, K., Malderez, A., Pell, G., Simm, C. and Johnson, F. (2004) *Why people choose to become teachers and the factors influencing their choice of ITT route: early findings from the Becoming a Teacher (BaT) Project*. Nottingham: Department for Education and Skills (DfES) (Research Brief). Available at www.dfes.gov.uk/research/data/uploadfiles/RBX08-04.pdf

Hobson, A. J., Malderez, A., Tracey, L. and Pell, G. (2006) 'Pathways and stepping stones: student teachers' preconceptions and concerns about initial teacher preparation in England', *Scottish Educational Review*, 37 (Special Issue on Teacher Education and Development), 59–78.

Hobson, A. J., Malderez, A., Tracey, L., Giannakaki, M. S., Pell, R. G. and Tomlinson, P. D. (2008) 'Student teachers' experiences of initial teacher preparation in England: core themes and variation', *Research Papers in Education*, 23 (4), 407–433.

Hobson, A. J., Malderez, A., Tracey, L., Homer, M., Mitchell, N., Biddulph, M., Giannakaki, M. S., Rose, A., Pell, R. G., Chambers, G. N., Roper, T. and Tomlinson, P. D. (2007) *Newly Qualified Teachers' experiences of their first year of teaching: Findings from Phase III of the Becoming a Teacher project*. Nottingham: Department for Children, Schools and Families (DCSF). Available at www.dfes.gov.uk/research/data/upload-files/DCSF-RR008%20v2.pdf.

Malderez, A., Hobson, A. J., Tracey, L. and Kerr, K. (2007), 'Becoming a student teacher: core features of the experience', *European Journal of Teacher Education*, 30 (3), 225–248.

Finally, if you want to learn more about educational and social research in general, we recommend the following introductory texts:

Bryman, A. (2008, third edition) *Social Research Methods*. Oxford: Oxford University Press.

Wellington, J. (2000) *Educational Research: Contemporary Issues and Practical Approaches*. London: Continuum.

Glossary

Higher education institutions (HEIs) Universities or colleges of higher education that offer programmes of undergraduate and/or postgraduate study. HEIs that administer programmes of ITT (see below) are sometimes referred to as ITT providers (see below).

Initial teacher training (ITT) programme A programme leading to formal qualification as a teacher; also known as 'initial teacher education' (ITE), 'pre-service (teacher) training', 'initial teacher education and training' (ITET) and 'initial teacher preparation' (ITP).

ITT providers Institutions, normally HEIs (see above) or schools, that administer and provide programmes of initial teacher training (see above).

Newly qualified teacher (NQT) A term generally used to describe teachers in their first year in post after successfully completing a programme of ITT (see above). In England, the term NQT refers specifically to teachers who are following a statutory Induction programme designed to enable them to meet a set of NQT Standards that build on the Standards for ITT (see below). The Induction period normally lasts for one school year of full time teaching.

Office for Standards in Education (Ofsted) The official government body in England that is responsible for the monitoring and inspection of schools.

Primary schools/primary phase (of education) These terms refer (in England) to schools that cater for (or teachers who teach) children within the 4–11 age range. Within the primary phase of education there are 'infant' (4- to 7-year-olds) and 'junior' (7–11) sections, sometimes within the same school and sometimes in different schools. (See 'Secondary schools' below.)

Pupils Learners, and the primary recipients of teaching, in schools. We have chosen not to refer to these as 'students' to avoid potential confusion with 'student teachers' (see below) or other students in HEIs (see above).

Qualified Teacher Status (QTS) The professional accreditation needed in order to teach in state-maintained schools in England (and Wales). This is generally attained through undertaking a period of

ITT (see above) and demonstrating that a set of Standards (see below) has been met.

Secondary schools/secondary phase   These terms, as used in England, refer to schools for (or teachers who teach) children within the 11–16 or 11–18 age range. (See 'Primary schools' above.)

Special Measures   Schools in England designated as being in 'Special Measures' are those that, according to inspectors of the Office for Standards in Education (see above), are 'failing to provide an acceptable standard of education', and in which the school leadership is 'not demonstrating the capacity to secure the necessary improvement in the school' (Education Act 2005).

Standards   The QTS Standards in England outline the skills, knowledge and understanding student teachers need to demonstrate they have achieved in order to be awarded Qualified Teacher Status (see above).

Student teacher   Someone enrolled on an ITT programme. Also known as a 'trainee', 'trainee teacher', 'learner teacher', 'student' or 'intern'.

Teachers of teachers (ToTs)   Staff working on ITT programmes, in schools, universities and/or other institutions, whose job (at least in part) is to support the learning of student teachers. Includes people variously referred to as teacher educators, teacher trainers, cooperating teachers, supervisors, mentors, induction tutors, ITT coordinators, tutors and lecturers!

Teaching practice   Commonly refers to that period (or those periods) of an ITT course (see above) when student teachers undergo extensive school-based experience. Also known as the 'practicum', 'teaching placement' or 'teaching experience' components of an ITT programme. Usually used to describe aspects of university- or college-administered programmes, rather than of employment-based or school-based programmes.

Trainee/trainee teacher   Also known as student teacher (see above).

Workload Agreement   A national agreement, reached in 2003 between the government, teachers' unions and other stakeholders in England and Wales, to introduce a series of measures designed to address and reduce teacher workload. The measures, phased in from 2003 to 2005, include a reduction in the number of administrative tasks teachers should be asked to undertake, the employment of more support staff to undertake some of those tasks, a limit on the number of times teachers are required to cover for absent colleagues, and the introduction of protected preparation, planning and assessment (PPA) time, equivalent to 10 per cent of teachers' timetabled school day.

Notes

Introduction

1 The terms 'student teacher', 'trainee teacher' and 'trainee' are used interchangeably to describe those following ITT programmes.

2 See, for instance, the work of Feiman-Nemser (2001) in the USA and Korthagen and colleagues (2001) in the Netherlands.

3 The 'Becoming a Teacher' research project (2003–2009) was funded by the Department for Education and Skills (DfES), the General Teaching Council (GTC) and the Training and Development Agency for Schools (TDA) in England. The student teachers that we spoke to and who took part in the survey were following a range of different types of ITT programme in England, including undergraduate and postgraduate university-administered programmes, school-centred and employment-based programmes. More information on the specific pathways into teaching that our research participants had followed is provided in the introduction to Chapter 2.

1 'I just fancied the challenge'

1 Whenever we provide a quotation from a student teacher in our research, as we do here, we give their gender and age and state whether they were training to teach in the primary or the secondary school sector.

2 In England these currently include the PGCE/Cert Ed in Further Education, and the Level 5 Diploma in Teaching in the Lifelong Learning Sector. For further details see www.learndirect-advice.co.uk/.

2 'It was the easiest and the quickest!'

1 Some of these questions may not be applicable to readers in countries where there are few or no ITT route options.

2 For these quotations, for clarity and further information, we have added the ITT route the student teacher was following, in addition to their gender, age group and whether they were seeking to teach in primary or in secondary schools.

3 We discuss the issue of workload further in Chapters 3 and 4, where we offer some advice on how to manage a heavy workload and achieve an appropriate work–life balance.

3 'You build teachers up into these god-like people who are fantastic and amazing and how will you ever be that perfect?'

1 In England, passing centrally assessed skills tests in numeracy, literacy and ICT are requirements for all student teachers prior to achieving Qualified Teacher Status (QTS). Similar tests are in place in some other systems, for example in certain states in the USA.

2 Eeyore, the donkey character in A. A. Milne's *Winnie-the-Pooh* books, is renowned for his gloomy outlook and for always seeing the glass as 'half-empty' rather than 'half-full'.

3 We are saving that advice which relates to obtaining your first teaching post to Section 3 (Chapter 9).

4 'It's all a bit overwhelming at first!'

1 We say 'most trainees' because some of you may have previously worked as (unqualified) teachers, though this is not to say that those of you in this position will not experience any shift in roles and/or identity during your ITT.

2 Incidentally, this (then) trainee was still a teacher four years after completing his ITT.

5 'It wears you down emotionally'

1 For this and other approaches, see Porter (2000) cited at the end of this chapter.

2 You might like to look at Alan Maley's *The Language Teacher's Voice* (2000), which suggests ways all teachers (not just language teachers) can look after the important tool that is their voice, and ways in which you can use your voice more effectively (particularly but not only in language teaching).

6 'All the theory goes out of the window'?

1 This 'five-step' process is presented and explained in Malderez and Wedell (2007).

7 'I'm glad I've built up such good relationships'

1 Dörnyei and Murphey's book *Group Dynamics in the Language Classroom* (2003) is a useful source of ideas and strategies for managing this aspect of our work. Many are relevant to all teachers, not only language teachers.

8 'I can't be doing with it'

1 Adapted from a story in Owen (2001).

9 'I just got this feeling when I walked in; I felt that I would fit there'

1 Schools in England designated as being in 'Special Measures' are those that, according to inspectors of the Office for Standards in Education (Ofsted), are 'failing to provide an acceptable standard of education', and where 'the persons responsible for leading, managing or governing the school are not demonstrating the capacity to secure the necessary improvement in the school' (Education Act 2005).

2 The Workload Agreement refers to a national (2003) agreement in England, signed by the government and teachers' unions, to move towards reducing teachers' workloads through, for example, employing more support staff. (See Glossary for more information.)

Appendix

1 The national profile of student teachers was derived from the Teacher Training Agency's Performance Profile data for 2003.

References

Argyle, M. (1969) *Social Interaction*. London: Methuen.

Bennett, T. (2008) 'Master class', *Times Educational Supplement*, 27 June.

Bubb, S. and Early, P. (2004) *Managing Teacher Workload: Worklife Balance and Wellbeing*. California: Paul Chapman.

Capel, S. (2001) 'Secondary students' development as teachers over the course of a PGCE year', *Educational Research*, 43 (3), 247–261.

Claxton, G. (1989) *Being a Teacher: A Positive Approach to Change and Stress*. London: Cassell.

Claxton, G. (1997) *Hare Brain, Tortoise Mind: Why Intelligence Increases When You Think Less*. London: Fourth Estate.

Csikszentmihalyi, M. (1990) *Flow: The Psychology of Optimal Experience*. New York: Harper and Row.

Dillon, J. and Maguire, M. (Eds) (2007) *Becoming a Teacher: Issues in Secondary Teaching*. Maidenhead: Open University Press.

Dörnyei, Z. and Murphey, T. (2003) *Group Dynamics in the Language Classroom*. Cambridge: Cambridge University Press.

Education Act (2005). Available at: www.opsi.gov.uk/ACTS/acts2005/ukpga_20050018_en_1 (accessed 12 November 2008).

Edwards, A. and Ogden, L. (1998) 'Mentoring as protecting the performance of student teachers', paper presented at the Annual Conference of the American Educational Research Association, San Diego, CA, April.

Feiman-Nemser, S. (2001), 'Helping novices learn to teach', *Journal of Teacher Education*, 52 (1), 17–30.

Glasser, W. (1998) *Choice Theory*. New York: HarperCollins.

Gootman, M. E. (2001) *The Caring Teacher's Guide to Discipline: Helping Young Students Learn Self-control, Responsibility and Respect*. Thousand Oaks, CA: Corwin.

Heron, J. (1989) *The Facilitator's Handbook*. London: Kogan Page.

Humphreys, T. (1998) *A Different Kind of Discipline*. Dublin: Newleaf.

Kagan, D. M. (1992) 'Professional growth among pre-service and beginning teachers', *Review of Educational Research*, 62 (2), 129–169.

Korthagen, F. A. J., Kessels, J., Koster, B., Lagerwerf, B. and Wubbels, T. (2001) *Linking Practice and Theory: The Pedagogy of Realistic Teacher Education*. Mahwah, New Jersey: Lawrence Erlbaum Associates.

Malderez, A. and Wedell, M. (2007) *Teaching Teachers: Processes and Practices*. London: Continuum.

Maley, A. (2000) *The Language Teacher's Voice*. Oxford: Macmillan Heinemann.

Oberski, I., Ford, K., Higgins, S. and Fisher, P. (1999) 'The importance of relationships in teacher education', *Journal of Education for Teaching*, 25 (2), 135–50.

Owen, N. (2001) *The Magic of Metaphor: 77 Stories for Teachers, Trainers and Thinkers*. Carmarthen, Wales: Crown House Publishing.

Porter, L. (2000) *Behaviour in Schools: Theory and Practice for Teachers*. Buckingham: Open University Press.

Index

academic element of programmes 62
altruistic motivation 16–17
application and appointment process,
    preparation for 137–8
appropriate behaviour, modeling of
    83
Argyle, M. 110
assessment of learning, development
    of skills in 39
assistance, sources of 119–20
attractiveness of teaching 13, 14,
    16–19
authoritarianism 81–2
available teaching posts, finding out
    about 137

*Becoming a Teacher: Issues in
    Secondary Teaching* (Dillon, J. and
    Maguire, M., eds) 90
beginning ITT 6, 55–74; academic
    element of programmes 62;
    building on strengths 63;
    confidence boost of supportive
    mentoring 70–1; confidence in
    ITT preparation for teaching 73;
    context of placement schools 61;
    coping strategies 67–9; cumulative
    phases in learning 65–6; demands
    of 55; early experiences, nature
    of 55; early highs 69–72;
    emotional roller-coaster 55–6;
    ethos of placement schools 61;
    family and friends, support from
    72; family considerations 57–8;
    fellow trainees, satisfactions in
    support from 72; finding the
    teacher within 62–3; frustrations
    in early experiences 56–67;
    joy of 'seeing' learning happen

69–70; long-term goal, focus
    on 72–3; looking after yourself
    68–9; mentors, satisfactions in
    support from 70–1; mentors and
    other teachers, relationships with
    63–6; mistakes, inevitability of
    67; noticing skills, development
    of 59–60; observation period,
    difficulties of 58–60; personal
    well-being 68–9; phases in
    learning, cumulative nature of
    65–6; planning, importance of
    (and planning for the unplanned)
    67–8; positive relations with
    other teachers 71–2; pressures
    of 56; pupil behaviour 65, 66;
    relationships with pupils 66;
    rewards of 69–72; role-shift,
    coping with 61–2; school staff,
    satisfactions in support from
    71–2; social life, impact on 57–8;
    structures in placement schools
    61; teaching skills, observation
    to develop 60; theoretical aspects
    of programmes, relevance of
    65, 66–7; time management,
    importance of 57–8; transition
    to teacher role, difficulties of
    61–3; unplanned, planning for
    67–8; unwelcoming placement
    schools 65; work–life balance,
    achievement of 57–8; worries
    about early experiences 56–67
behaviour: choices of, importance
    of understanding 88–9; expected
    behaviour, modelling of 87;
    expected behaviour, personal
    perspectives on 77; in-class
    behaviour, learning about 45;